THE *Silent* WARRIOR

How my wife overcame her adversities

RICHARD BRYAN ASHFORD

THE

Silent
WARRIOR

How my wife overcame her adversities

RICHARD BRYAN ASHFORD

ISBN# 978-1-935075-79-0

Printed in the United States of America.

Printed by Calvary Publishing
A Ministry of Parker Memorial Baptist Church
1902 East Cavanaugh Road
Lansing, Michigan 48910
www.CalvaryPublishing.org

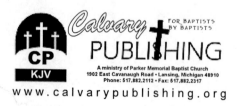

Calvary PUBLISHING
FOR BAPTISTS BY BAPTISTS
CP KJV
A ministry of Parker Memorial Baptist Church
1902 East Cavanaugh Road • Lansing, Michigan 48910
Phone: 517.882.2112 • Fax: 517.882.2317
www.calvarypublishing.org

CONTENTS

INTRODUCTION

This is how my wife's faith overcame her trials and tribulations and turned them into victories. As you read these stories on how Satan tried to destroy her life and our family, you will read how Charlotte turned to God for strength and to the Bible for wisdom. You will see how she earned the name Silent Warrior. As you read her story, stop and read each scripture, for in those scriptures you will find the secret on how to overcome and defeat Satan and his angels. May God Bless you in your Christian walk, and give you strength and wisdom in your battles.

one

CHARLOTTE GOES TO JAIL!

-- *1954-1970* --

Charlotte was born on February 28th, 1954 in Amarillo Texas. It was a cold dreary Sunday morning at 11:00 a.m. This was one of the few Sundays that Mama ever missed; you can count on one hand the Sundays Charlotte's mom missed church. This will play a big part in the years of setting an example for Charlotte of never missing church.

That was the day Charlotte was born into a loving family that cherished their new baby daughter. Charlotte came 11 and 13 years later than her sister and brother. Things were good for a while. Life at first seemed to be normal. But that was short lived! Even as a baby Charlotte began to see that something was not right. One of her first memories of her daddy was watching him drink whiskey from the bottle and the pain on her daddy's face as he drank it straight. It looked like it hurt; and she could not understand why he would not stop hurting himself.

> "Wine *is* a mocker, strong drink *is* raging: and who-soever is deceived thereby is not wise."
>
> **Proverbs 20:1**

One day she was about 9 to 10 months old when she crawled to a closet door that was open and saw a bottle of whiskey hidden inside. Charlotte looked up at her mom and said, "Da-Da!" And people think they are only hurting themselves when they drink. They are starting to influence their children at an age before they can even walk. They are setting their children up for failure! It is hard enough to battle Satan outside of your home. But to invite Satan in! All I want to say here is "Dads and Moms wake up!" The sin that you live will be your families down fall! The old saying is you play with fire, you get burned, but it doesn't stop there; your loved one will get burned too.

> "No man can serve two masters: for either he will hate the one, and love the other; or else he will hold to the one, and despise the other. Ye cannot serve God and mammon."
>
> **Matthew 6:24**

But Charlotte had good memories mixed with bad ones. When she was 2 years old, her brother would pick on her. Her brother would put his hands on the top of Charlotte's head and push her down to the ground but Charlotte would always stand right back up laughing and ready for more. You will see later in Charlotte's life how her Christian walk was molded by her childhood. You will see how her mom, brother and sister and even her dad had a part in making and molding who she is today.

When Charlotte was just 3 and 4 years old, she would watch Popeye on black and white TV. Popeye was always getting beat up by Brutus, everywhere Popeye went he would run into Brutus and get beat up time and time again. But Popeye had a secret; it was his spinach that he had hidden in his shirt. And just when Popeye was about to be defeated he would eat his spinach and get strong and then he would beat up Brutus and make him run off scared.

Charlotte always had that big can of spinach in her shirt, just like Popeye. She would walk around looking for Brutus, ready for a fight. She never was scared of him because she had her secret weapon with her, but it's not spinach anymore, it's her Bible, and she's not looking for Brutus, she's looking for Satan and through the Power of God, she's ready for battle.

"For the word of God *is* quick, and powerful, and sharper than any twoedged sword, piercing even to the dividing asunder of soul and spirit, and of the joints and marrow, and *is* a discerner of the thoughts and intents of the heart."

Hebrews 4:12

"I have fought a good fight, I have finished *my* course,
I have kept the faith:"

2 Timothy 4:7

There were times that she would watch cartoons with her brother and sister and they would laugh and the good guys always won. They watched cartoons like, Mighty Mouse, and sang that song *"Here I come to save the day."* Then there was Rough and Redi, *"Here comes Rough and Redi, Here comes Rough and Redi."* There was Yogi the Bear and Boo Boo and Huckleberry Hound Dog, Quick Draw McGraw, Davy and Goliath, Woody Woodpecker and Felix the Cat *"The wonderful wonderful cat, you laugh so much your side will ache, your heart will go pit-ter-pat, watch Felix the wonderful cat."*

Then there was good days with her dad and they would play baseball and work outside in the yard together, painting the house, mowing the yard together and going to get ice cream. They would watch Gunsmoke together. And her dad would laugh when his little girl would stand in front of the TV with her gun holster and did her Matt Dillon impression where his knee twitched just right before his first draw. Her dad was proud of her being that young and seeing his knee twitch. Then there were the days of her daddy working with wood and lacquer at Globe Refinery. They would pick him up from work and she could smell the lacquer and wood. She loved the smell of his clothes.

Those were the good days. But those days soon only became memories. As the drinking became more and more, Charlotte began to see less and less of her dad. There were times when he would stay drunk for 2 weeks at a time and not come home. Charlotte told me of a time when she was 4 years old and she saw her daddy getting ready to leave the house to go drink again. So she latched on to his leg and clung to him and bit his leg as if she was trying to keep him home. But in the end, alcohol won again.

The promises to stop drinking became just words with no meaning. The drinking became more and more. He could not hold down a job anymore. Mama was the only source of money that was coming in. She cleaned houses and barely made minimum wage; they never missed a meal or rent payments. With what little money that did come in, God was watching over them.

Charlotte wore a lot of hand-me-downs. And only had a few dresses. But she always held her head up and never let someone make fun of her. One day at school a mean girl that found out Charlotte came 13 years later, told her that she was an accident. Charlotte looked her in the eyes and said, *"I was not an accident, I was a surprise!"*

There it is, that fighting spirit of Charlotte, and in the near future Satan is going to hate that about her.

The drinking got worse, and with drinking came trouble, with the marriage and with the law. The law did not put up with him like Mama did all those years. When her dad got caught drinking and driving, they put him in county jail. The first time, Charlotte was only 3 years old. That was just one of many times that he ended up in county jail.

Every Saturday morning Charlotte would go to jail to see her dad. They would not let her go inside. So the only way was to look up at the barred windows and see her dad wave at her. She was so happy to see her daddy; she would jump up and down waving back. She loved her daddy.

> "The LORD hath appeared of old unto me, *saying,*
> Yea, I have loved thee with an everlasting love: therefore with lovingkindness have I drawn thee."
> **Jeremiah 31:3**

And anybody that walked by, she would tell them, *"That's my Daddy."* She learned then at such a young age to *"love the person, but hate the sin."*

But even the love of a daughter would not stop him from drinking. He was ordered by the courts to go to Alcoholic's Anonymous. Charlotte saw her dad many times get up in front of the A.A. crowd and talk, but he would never say I am an Alcoholic. He would say I'm J.D. Little and I have an alcoholic problem.

The drinking never stopped and the many months that were spent in jail kept adding up. When Charlotte turned 9 years old, the courts had enough with his drinking and driving. No longer were the days of driving to the courthouse to see her dad. The judge told her dad that for the next 4 years he will be sentenced to Huntsville State Prison. With what little money coming in, it was not possible to drive down to see her dad anymore. Charlotte was heartbroken. But as they drove her dad off to prison she told him. "No matter what I will always be here waiting for you when you come home."

The letters came and went, always promising Charlotte that he would not ever drink again. With good behavior her Daddy came home after 2 years. And Charlotte with all of her heart believed her Daddy was going to never drink again. That promise lasted one week and he was back to drinking again. But Charlotte still loved her Daddy.

With her Dad finally home from prison, the hope and dreams of everything "Now" was going to be ok. Her Dad promised his little girl that he would even go to church. It was Father's Day that Sunday and true to his word he went with Charlotte and

Momma. With her Mom sitting to her left and her Dad to her right, she felt for the first time in a long time like a real family.

The Pastor was preaching on the Romans Road that morning. For the last three Sundays, the Holy Spirit was convicting Charlotte to step out and walk to the altar and accept Christ as her Saviour, but fear held her back. But that Sunday was different; her Dad was there. And as the Holy Spirit began to convict her again, Charlotte's Dad looked down at his beautiful little daughter and said: *"Honey, if you want to go down to the altar, I will go with you."* That was all it took, the fear that held her back for so many weeks was gone. As she held her daddy's hand, they both went down to that old tear stained altar. As she prayed, Charlotte began to remember what her mom once said in Proverbs 3:5-6 – **"Trust in the LORD with all thine heart; and lean not unto thine own understanding. In all thy ways acknowledge him, and he shall direct thy paths."**

The Pastor came down from the pulpit and put his arms around her shoulder and showed Charlotte in the Bible how God will never let you down, how God's love is everlasting and that He will never leave you nor forsake you. All you have to do is accept that love of God's Son who died on the Cross in your place, for your sins. Then confess your sins and ask Jesus into your heart. The pastor began to explain that God is perfect and cannot allow sin into Heaven and we need Jesus as our mediator. Jesus Christ came down and lived a perfect and sinless life. And through Him we can have forgiveness and eternal life. So that day on Father's Day, Charlotte asked Jesus to forgive her of her sins and come into her heart and to be her Lord and Saviour. And on July 4th Charlotte was baptized. But little did she know that in the days to come, she would have to lean on and trust in God and His word. Proverbs 3:5-6 – **"Trust in the LORD with all thine heart; and lean not unto thine own understanding. In all thy ways acknowledge him, and he shall direct thy paths."**

One day close to Christmas, Charlotte saw something in the closet that she had always wanted. It was a Po-Go Stick. The excitement of having something from her dad was insurmountable. Christmas was coming soon. All of the hurt of those years faded away just thinking about it. The day before Christmas, Charlotte saw her dad pulling the Po-Go stick out of the closet and giving it to her cousin, to impress his sister. Charlotte faded back into her room and cried and cried.

When the hurting and the tears dried up; Charlotte got up and washed her face, never letting her dad see the hurt or tears. He never knew how bad he hurt her. In her heart she forgave him, and still loved him.

The years went by, but the alcohol and women were taking a toll on the marriage. Both Charlotte and Momma thought a little time with her dad was better than no dad at all. So it became the norm to only see her dad once in a while. But the weeks got longer and days shorter in seeing her dad. But Charlotte began to see something else wrong, even when he was sober he did not come home anymore. And one day after school, hoping to see her dad at home, bad news struck again. Her dad wanted a divorce; he found another womon that had money. At first there was anger from both her mom and her. Then came the tears. Charlotte told me, it was as if he had died; it was as if he divorced Charlotte too. No more dad, he did not like his old life, so he traded it in for a new life. And let the chips fall where they may. Except the chips were his family. But time heals, and life must go on.

> "Blessed *be* God, even the Father of our Lord Jesus Christ, the Father of mercies, and the God of all comfort; Who comforteth us in all our tribulation, that we may be able to comfort them which are in any trouble, by the comfort wherewith we ourselves are comforted of God."
>
> **2 Corinthians 1:3-4**

Charlotte began to get more and more involved in church. And God became her new dad. A dad that would never forsake or let her down.

"...for he hath said, I will never leave thee, nor forsake thee."

Hebrews 13:5

God became number 1 in her life. And God was always there. Just like the "Foot prints in the Sand."

Footprints in the Sand
*One night I dreamed I was walking along the beach
with the Lord.
Many scenes from my life flashed across the sky.
In each scene I noticed footprints in the sand.
Sometimes there were two sets of footprints,
Other times there were one set of footprints.
This bothered me because I noticed
That during the low periods of my life,
When I was suffering from
Anguish, sorrow or defeat,
I could see only one set of footprints.
So I said to the Lord,
"You promised me Lord,
That if I followed you,
You would walk with me always.
But I have noticed that during
The most trying periods of my life
There has only been one*

Set of footprints in the sand.
Why, when I needed you most,
You have not been there for me?"
The Lord replied,
"The times when you have
Seen only one set of footprints in the sand,
Is when I carried you!"

But there was one difference, Charlotte has never doubted where God was, and when trouble hits; Charlotte has always known God was carrying her. Charlotte, with her broken childhood will tell you today, God is the same today, yesterday and forever. God will never let you down.

"Trust in the LORD with all thine heart; and lean not unto thine own understanding. In all thy ways acknowledge him, and he shall direct thy paths."
Proverbs 3:5-6

Develop an Attitude of Gratitude

If you tend to gravitate toward what's negative in life rather than what's positive, begin praying: "Even though I clutch my blanket and growl when the alarm goes off, thank you Lord that I can hear; there are many who are deaf. Even though I close my eyes as long as possible against the morning light, thank you Lord that I can see; there are many who are blind. Even though I put off the effort to praise, thank you Lord that I have the strength to get up; there are many who are bedridden. Even though the first hour of my day is hectic when socks are lost, toast is burned and tempers are short, thank you Lord for my family; there are many who are alone. Even though our breakfast table never looks like pictures in the magazines and the menu at times is unbalanced, thank you Lord for the food we have; there are many who are hungry. Even though my job is sometimes monotonous, thank you for the opportunity to work; there are many who are unemployed. Even though I complain from time to time and wish my circumstances were different, thank you for the gift of life; there are people in the graveyard who would gladly change places with me. Even though I make mistakes, stumble and fall, thank you for the grace to get up again; there are many who didn't make it, thank you Lord for all these blessings and 101 others that I've taken for granted. Amen."

Author Unknown

"In every thing give thanks: for this is the will of God in Christ Jesus concerning you."

1 Thessalonians 5:18

Letter of Hope

No matter what our circumstances are, God's grace is sufficient. God can take our weakness and make it strong through His grace. God may not always change the circumstances of life, but God does promise us that whatever our problems are, He can give us the strength and power to keep them from destroying us. Having a problem is not as important as our reaction to it! Will we allow it to destroy us? Will we learn from it and become stronger Christians? Paul had a problem, he had prayed three times for God to remove it. Paul called it his "thorn in the flesh" God's answer was not to remove the "thorn in the flesh," but to give him an even better answer to his prayer. The answer was that God would give him strength and power through His grace, to live with his difficulty. He would be made stronger because of it.

God does not promise to change the circumstances of life we find difficult. What He does promise, is to give us the power and the strength to live in the circumstances we have. He promises to be with us in the midst of difficulty. Life cannot defeat us as long as God is with us!

Marquita Lenerose (Charlotte's Sister)

"And he said unto me, My grace is sufficient for thee: for my strength is made perfect in weakness. Most gladly therefore will I rather glory in my infirmities, that the power of Christ may rest upon me. Therefore I take pleasure in infirmities, in reproaches, in necessities, in persecutions, in distresses for Christ's sake: for when I am weak, then am I strong."

2 Corinthians 12: 9-10

Two

THE GIRL OF MY DREAMS

-------1972----------

When I turned 16 years old, I began to want what the world offered. I began to listen to the wrong kind of music and believe what I saw on TV and the movies. They showed a life of fun and freedom with no consequences. Up until then my dad and mom made sure I went to church and even sent me to a Christian School for 4 years. I became a Christian at age 9, at a Revival. The preacher that night was a man named Tommy Phelps [Nature Boy], an ex-wrestler turned evangelist. But even as a child of God, I began to wander, I became just like the Prodigal son mentioned in the Bible. *[Luke 15:11-24]* I knew what it was like being an obedient child of God with all the Rules and Commandments that I had to follow every day. But Satan kept whispering in my ear that if I would just follow him, I would be free, no more rules and no more guilt and I fell for it. I began to lust after the things of the world. All I cared about was what I wanted. Nothing and nobody else mattered but me. But when I began to see the true emptiness of the world and that Satan is a liar and a deceiver, I wanted out.

John 8:44 **"Ye are of your father the devil, and the lusts of your father ye will do. He was a murderer from the beginning, and abode not in the truth, because there is no truth in him. When he speaketh a lie, he speaketh of his own: for he is a liar, and the father of it."**

But when you fall into temptation and the sin of this world and under the power of Satan, you cannot escape his grip on your own. I began to pray to God for help; I wanted to come back home to the protection of God. I did not like what I saw of the end results of what Satan does to people when he is through with them. The unhappiness that looking for hope and love that Satan promised them and didn't provide; you could see the loneliness and pain in their eyes which told it all.

Gal 5:17 **" For the flesh lusteth against the Spirit, and the Spirit against the flesh: and these are contrary the one to the other: so that ye cannot do the things that ye would."**

Gal 5:19 – 21a **"Now the works of the flesh are manifest, which are these; Adultery, fornication, uncleanness, lasciviousness, Idolatry, witchcraft, hatred, variance, emulations, wrath,**

strife, seditions, heresies, Envyings, murders, drunkenness, revellings, and such like: ..."

The hold that Satan had on me felt like I was his puppet and every time that Satan said jump, I jumped. I wanted those ropes cut and to be released from that power. As I began to pray that God would send someone into my life to help me, God allowed me to begin to dream of my future wife. God allowed me to see that if I would just let go of the world and come back to Him, that someday He would bless me with this beautiful girl of my dreams. I began to seek after the will of God in my life. As the days and months went by, the lust of the world and Satan began to lose the grip it had on me.

I began to want to go to church again, but wasn't sure where. When a child of God gets out of God's will, it messes our minds up. So I began to try to find out what church God wanted me to go to. I'll never forget this one church that I went to. The first thing you do when you walk inside is drink some wine they had at the back and say some kind of prayer and then go sit down. And when the priest walks by, you kneel down and stay on your knees until he passes.

Psalm 95:6 **"O come, let us worship and bow down: let us kneel before the LORD our maker."**

I had enough sense to know you do not bow down before man, only God. They told me I had to kneel and I refused. That's when several Deacons came by and escorted me out of that church. As I was walking back to the car, I thought to myself, "God does not want me going to this church."

The next week I went to another kind of church that had almost the same kind of wine cup, so I thought I knew what to do. I picked up what I thought was a bowl of wine and drank it. As I began to swallow, my taste buds began to scream out, "this is not wine" ,and it tasted like 1000 dirty fingers. I began to spit out what was left in my mouth and let out a yell of "what is this!" As it turned out, it was Holy Water and you were suppose to dip your fingers in it "not drink it". Even today I can still remember the taste of that finger water. "YUK"

The Priest came running toward me with several other men and literally kicked me out the door. I thought to myself, I guess God does not want me in this church either.

That year was a battle with Satan pulling me one way and God pulling me another way. I was praying one night that God would let me meet this girl of my dreams. I needed to just see if she was real or not. I made a promise to God that I would get my life together if I could marry this girl of my dreams. God saw that I was trying, so that week my dreams became reality.

I was working that summer at an amusement

park and I will never forget what happened next. I was running the bumper cars, when I looked up; there she was walking about 10 feet away with this little boy beside her. The girl of my dreams was walking right by me. She never looked up, she was saying something to that little boy she had with her. I was in total shock, she did not look a little like the girl of my dreams, she was the girl of my dreams. I just stood in shock as she walked by. When I came to my senses I yelled at this kid I knew that I went to school with. I asked him to run and tell that girl I wanted to talk to her. I pointed her out as she was leaving; he said he would go tell her. About 5 minutes later he came back and said she drove off before he could catch her. I was heartbroken. He asked me if I knew her. "No," I said, but I wanted to. My friend said that he knew her sister and that he was their paperboy. I asked, not that it mattered, but I wanted to know if that was her kid. He said no, it was her sister's kid. Then I asked if he knew her name, he said no but her sister's name is Marquita. That's when my friend's dad yelled out it was time to go. I never found out anything else about the girl of my dreams. Only that she was real and God allowed me to see her. That would be the last time I saw her. Every time I was outside, I would look for her; hundreds of faces I would see and none of them were her.

My dreams of her went from once a month to

every week. God knew my life was not cleaned up enough for her. But those 10 seconds of seeing her was what I needed to put a fire under me. Each day I prayed and read my Bible. I believed that if I kept my promise that God would keep His. Each church I went to, I would look for her. One day I went to this church that had an altar call and everybody went up in front and prayed out loud. So I went up next to these girls my age and listened to them pray and confessd their sins. And "wow" the things that they confess to, that they did that week. My flesh and Satan told me that this is the church for you. As I got up from the altar I was met by one of the girls dads. He told me to leave and not come back. And again, I knew God's will was not that church.

Another year went by and I could not find where God wanted me. No matter where I went I never saw that girl in my dreams again. Church after church that I went to, something always happened, either I was asked to leave or the preaching did not feed my soul. I would leave more spiritually hungry than when I went in. But something strange was happening to me; I was beginning to not desire the things of this world anymore. I began to desire God's truth and wisdom.

All this time my parents were praying for me to find my way back to God's will. They started going to this little Baptist church and fell in love with the pastor and the people. About this time, I gave up trying to find the right church. My parents asked the youth director to go visit me and try to get me back in church. Come to find out the youth director was my old football coach from the Christian school I went to. My parents must have been forewarned, because when the door bell rang, I looked around and they both vanished. So as I went to the door to see who it was, I stopped by the window and looked out and saw my old football coach and about 8 young people with him.

As I opened the door to see what they wanted, I could not believe what I saw! I just stood there in shock; my first thought was that I was dreaming again. As I was opening the door, the first face I saw was my old football coach, then this girl stepped out from behind him. I could not believe who I was looking at, the girl of my dreams. To this day I have no idea what my old coach said to me. All I heard was, "Would you like to come to Sunday school?" I could not keep my eyes off of her. I asked if they wanted to come in, so one by one they filled up my living room. The youth director began to introduce everybody to me, but I only heard one name, Charlotte Little. As Charlotte sat down she saw a newspaper clipping that had my name in it. It was an article about me and my dad riding our bikes over 300 miles. And again I never heard what the coach said to me, I only heard Charlotte say "WOW" after she read the article.

Here sat the girl of my dreams and the last time I saw her was a year and a half ago. And the first time I heard her speak and she said "WOW"; my first thoughts were to ask her to marry me! But God was not finished with me yet; I had a lot of maturing and growing spiritually to do. God had kept His promise and I was going to keep mine. I turned back to my old coach and he was still talking, his mouth was moving but I only heard the words, "Will you come to Sunday school?" By now you know what my answer was; I looked up at Charlotte and said "YES!!! I will be there!" Charlotte smiled and then everybody got up and left. I watched her walk away and get into a van and drive off. I sat back down and my heart was still beating fast, the girl of dreams said "WOW" and smiled at me. My thoughts were she loves me! The truth is, I loved her but her love for me came much later. For the next year I never missed a church service.

Three

CHARLOTTE FIRE BOMBS A CAR

-- 1973 --

I was sitting in my high school class when over the intercom my name was being announced *"Richard Ashford, report to Amarillo Police Department immediately!"* I began to think that since I met Charlotte; I have done nothing wrong. So when I stood up to leave, I could hear people talking about me, saying I wonder what he did this time. And I was wondering too.

I showed up at the front desk at the Amarillo Police Department and told them my name. She said we have been waiting for you. And the next thing I knew I was being told to go with this detective.

He told me to go inside this little room and sit and stay. This room was about a 4' x 4' and had 2 chairs and a table, and a big light hanging over my head. When he left, he locked the door behind him. I tried to think what I did, but could not come up with anything. Since I met Charlotte, I turned my life over to Christ and was trying to get my act together.

As I was waiting for the detective to come back, minutes turned into hours and hours turned into days. It felt like an eternity, in the hot lights, the hard chair and the little boxed in room. Finally the detective came back, I looked at my watch and it had only been 45 minutes, since he left. He looked at me and told me I could go now! I said, *"What do you mean, I can go now?"* What was all this about? So he began to tell me about this car that was firebombed last night and that there was an eyewitness that said that Charlotte and I called him up and threatened him. And then came over that night and fire bombed his parent's car.

I told the detective we had nothing to do with the firebombing of anybody's car. He said, *"I know, I just got through talking to your dad. Your dad was out on patrol and I had him to come in and talk to me. I asked him, "Could Richard have fire bombed that car?" Your dad said, "Yes, he could have, but I don't know if he did."* The detective went on to say that this eye witness also saw Charlotte with your son, firebombing this car. My dad stood up and looked this detective in the eyes and said, *"If Charlotte had anything to do with this, he would lay his badge down and quit."* Charlotte would not do anything like this. She is one the strongest Christian girls I have ever met. The detective asked my dad, *"Then this eyewitness is lying?"* My dad said, *"You bet he is lying!"* And that is when the detective came back and told me that I could leave.

As I walked out of the Police Station I began to think that because of Charlotte's testimony, I was set free. I wanted to someday work hard and serve God and have a testimony likeCharlotte.

> "A *good* name is rather to be chosen than great riches, *and* loving favour rather than silver and gold."
> **Proverbs 22:1**

When I got home I called up Charlotte and asked her, "Did you have to go down to the Police Station?" She said, No! Why? "I said because we were blamed in firebombing a car. So I told her what happened and we had a good laugh.

That night when I crawled into bed, I thanked God for Charlotte and her strong Christian testimony.

P.S. I guess you want to know who firebombed the car! About a year later the detective told us it was the eyewitness that did it. He went to the same church as we did. And he liked Charlotte and when I told him that if he ever asked Charlotte out on a date, I would beat him up. I told all the guys in that church that I would beat them up if they asked her out. I thought that if I eliminated all of my competition, that Charlotte someday would marry me! And it worked! This guy wanted to get back at me, so he firebombed. It would have worked if he had just blamed me.

four

USMC

-- 1980-1986 --

E ver since I married Charlotte, I wanted to serve my country and be a Marine. Charlotte has never stood in my way of me fulfilling my dreams. She has always backed me up and never thought of herself. My dreams became her dreams. So after 6 years of marriage, she looked at me one morning and said, *"When are you leaving?"* I asked her, *"What do you mean?"* She said, *"For the Marine Corps!"* At that time we were youth directors, and God was number one in both of our lives. So we both knew and trusted each other no matter how many miles apart.

So off I went to join the United States Marine Corps. I came home that night and said I am being shipped off in a couple of months, we were both so happy. I told Charlotte to pray that it would be the hardest boot camp ever. By now you know Charlotte; she went to all the ladies in the church to pray that it would be the toughest and the hardest boot camp ever.

That day soon came and it was time for me to leave. We were not sad, both of us were excited that I was going after a goal of mine. We kissed and hugged for a long time. I had an idea that at 10:00 pm Central Time, we would look up at the moon together. We said our goodbyes at the airport. I got on the plane and waved goodbye to her.

When I landed in San Diego, I was told to report to this Drill Instructor at the end of the terminal. I went into the bathroom to clean up a little and that was when I met several other recruits. They looked so scared and I could not imagine why. Then we all walked over to the Drill Instructor and introduced ourselves. He started yelling at us, calling us every name in the book. That was the start of total chaos. And chaos was an understatement.

We all loaded onto this bus and were told to sit and wait, with the windows closed and doors shut and breathing stale hot air. We all started to sweat and move around a little. That's when the Drill Instructor came back and started to yell at us again, telling us not to move or talk. Then he left again. I asked the guy next to me why he joined USMC. He looked at me with fear in his eyes and said that he was sick and tired of his parents telling him what to do all the time. I looked at him and started to laugh. Little did I know, that was going to be the last time I laughed, for the next 4 months there was no

more laughter heard, nothing was funny anymore.
It turned out to be just trying to survive each day;
taking one hour at a time, our days turned out to be
20 hour days with only 2 to 4 hours to rest. Back on
the bus we waited almost 4 hours for everybody to
fly in from different parts of the United States

God was going to break my spirit, so that I
would rely only on Him, and not myself. And while
God was breaking me, God was building up Charlotte to overcome her fears and to be a bolder witness for Christ.

> "For God hath not given us the spirit of fear; but of
> power, and of love, and of a sound mind."
> **2 Timothy 1:7**

We finally received enough on the bus to drive
to the USMC recruit Depo. That's when we met up
with more Marines yelling at us. Some said go left,
others said stop, some said go, what a mess. Here
were 80 of us running around in circles. Finally we
were told, to go to the yellow painted footprints
and don't move. After several hours of not moving
and standing at attention, our shoulders and legs
began to cramp up. If anybody moved, we were
hit and yelled at. Time seem to stop. We began to
think that the pain in our bodies was never going
to stop. But the pain was just beginning. We were

told after about 3 hours to run to this building and get our hair shaved off and then they threw us in these cold showers and told us to wash off all the civilian smell, and to go get our uniform, then run back to our barracks. That's when the beatings began. We were given 60 seconds to make our racks (beds) and of course nobody did it right, and so we were punished. We were told to go into the pits and be punished. The pits were nothing more than a big area outside. It's called the pit because of all the exercising and sweating that we did. We actually dug a small grave by turning that dirt into mud with our sweat. When the training officer yelled out "push-ups," we did pushups. And then yelled "mountain climbers," then yelled "sit ups," and then yelled out "bend 'n' thrust," then knee bends, we did every kind of exercise that night. After about 3 hours they said, "stop." It was about 0400 (4:00 am) and we were told time to go to bed. I was so happy to get some sleep. I was going to sleep until noon, I thought. At 0415 it was, "time to get up and start our day. We started off by running 5 miles for a warm up. Then back to the pit. By 0700 we were all exhausted. And we were told to line up and run to chow hall. We lined up and received our food and we were told we have 30 seconds to eat. By the time we got our food and sat down our time was up. About half of us did not get one bite.

This kind of treatment went on all day long. At lunch-time we lined up and received our chow but again only had 30 seconds again. And again half of us did not eat, and more running and punishment. It was still total chaos. Recruits were beaten and thrashed, telling us we could do nothing right. That night we did not get to the chow hall in time; so none of us ate. Weak and tired and around 2300 (11:00 p.m.) we made it back to our racks. We were ready for a good nights sleep, thinking maybe tomorrow would be better. Just when we thought sleep was near, they came in and told us to clean the floors and bathrooms with a toothbrush, after a lot of screaming and kicking us. We got through about 0200 (2:00 a.m.) Finally, we got to go to sleep. 0400s came early with only 2 hours of sleep. It started all over again.

But the yelling and chaos did not stop, each passing minute seemed like days. Time stood still. But we kept going day after day. Finally 30 days passed and I thought that I might make it after all. Then the news came that we were starting our training today. And that we were going to pick up our drill instructors. I thought we were in boot camp training already. We were in "receiving part" and none of those days counted.

So here we were in shock and starting the first day of boot camp. By now I have lost about 13 pounds from not eating. And now out of 80 marine corps boots we had already lost 8 men that had gotten hurt and could not continue. We thought it was bad before, but that was a cake walk compared to the pain and torture of what was ahead. All along I kept thinking and praying that Charlotte would quit praying that this would be the hardest boot camp ever. I would pray to God at night that He would not listen to Charlotte. But in the end, God heard Charlotte's prayers, not mine, God had something else planned for me, to break my pride and will.

> "A man's pride shall bring him low: but honour shall uphold the humble in spirit."
> **Proverbs 29:23**

The first day of boot camp, the drill instructors would not let us go to the head (restroom). For three days and two nights, I could hear moaning and crying all night long. They had the doors to the squad bay chained and locked. And had guards on the head so we could not sneak in and go. The pain was so bad at times that I felt like crying myself and just quit and try to escape. But the locked door and guards kept us from trying that idea out. It was the third night and the guards were gone and all of us must have noticed it at the same time. It was a mad rush.

Training was getting harder and harder. At night

this one guy tried to slit his wrist, he said he could not take it anymore, and wanted to die. They came and took him to the hospital. The next day one guy grabbed a bottle of Clorox and tried to drink it. When I turned around to look, it was the look of a guy that wanted out, no matter what the price it would bring. One guy was beat up so bad that they had to remove his spleen. Another guy tried jumping off of "Jacobs ladder" (a giant ladder made out of logs about 4 stories high) he broke both legs and an arm, he was in a full body cast. I will never forget what he said to me. I had asked him, *"What kind of dummy jumps off of Jacobs Ladder?"* He looked at me and smiled and said, *"I am going home and you're not!"* For about a second I thought he was not as dumb as I thought.

By now, we all looked like skeletons. Training was unbearable. We lost more and more recruits. Out of 80 guys that started we were down to about 60. My prayers began to change, I would pray to God at night and say to him, that I quit, I am in your hands. My future of me being a Marine is up to you. After a month I finally got time to write Charlotte and tell her to stop praying for this to be the hardest thing I have ever gone through. Also that I could not take it anymore, I just wanted to quit and come home.

Several days went by and I received a letter from

Charlotte. The letter read like this:

Dear Richard,

"Since you've gone to the pit so much; here are some scriptures that will help:

> "I waited patiently for the LORD; and he inclined unto me, and heard my cry. He brought me up also out of an horrible pit, out of the miry clay, and set my feet upon a rock, *and* established my goings. And he hath put a new song in my mouth, *even* praise unto our God: many shall see *it*, and fear, and shall trust in the LORD."
>
> **Psalms 40:1-3**

I know you're going through a hard time. And I am praying for you every minute of the day. This is what you have always dreamed of, so go for it. It's our dream and goal for you to be called a United States Marine. With God at your side. You will make it."

Yours forever, Love, Charlotte

When I read that letter I thought of this verse:

> "…If God *be* for us, who *can be* against us?"
>
> **Romans 8:31**

I bowed my head down and prayed this prayer,

"Dear Heavenly Father,

"I can do all things through Christ which strengtheneth me."

Philippians 4:13

I need you to give me the strength that Charlotte
has. The will to keep fighting. But most of all, to be
a good testimony of your Son, Jesus Christ, Amen."

When I stood up from that time on, I had the
power of God with me. The feeling sorry for myself
was gone. The true strength was in God's hands, not
mine; my life was no longer what I wanted in life but
what God wanted.

The days got harder and harder, more and more
wanted out, some tried to escape, but in the end they
always got caught. During Infantry training, we had
this one boot (recruit) that couldn't take the "Death
March." This was a march through the mountains,
up and down those mountains, hardly ever stopping
and getting little sleep. He turned to me and threw
his rifle to me and ran over to a cliff and jumped off.
He fell about 50 feet and then rolled about a hundred
yards and landed on a big boulder. It looked like he
broke his neck. They made us keep marching. About
30 minutes later I heard the medical helicopter flying
over our heads. Later that night, still climbing up and
down those hills, I heard whimpering and crying behind me about 200 yards away and two drill instruc-

tors yelling and kicking this boot back to us. I could not believe it, bruised up, but no broken bones, when he caught up to me, I gave him his rifle back and asked him if he was ok and why he tried to kill himself. He said he just wanted to break a bone or two, and go to the hospital so he could rest.

The next day one guy could not get his boots back on due to the blisters and swelling. So they made him walk with no boots. Within hours his feet were cut up so badly that they called in the medical helicopter to take him to the hospital. That morning a little rock got into my boot and by the end of the day when they let us stop, I could feel a big blister on my foot. But I dared not take my boot off; for fear that I could not get my boot back on. Three days later when infantry training was over and we came off that mountain and down to the barracks, that was when I took my boots off and had gangrene and cellulitus. They rushed me to the hospital and began cutting on my foot, with razor blades and knives. And all I could think about was, "this is nice." The doctors and nurses weren't yelling at me, people were smiling. The bed and pillows were so soft. I remembered praying that night, telling God, Thank You! For three days I slept and ate and wrote Charlotte a 10 page letter. It was so great; it was the best part of boot camp. With my strength back, I was ready to get back into training.

This one guy messed up his knees while climbing. And was told he would never walk again. By now we were down to only around 50 of us left. There were days that they would run us so hard that guys would pass out. They made us do sit ups on gravel roads, that stopped when they saw our backs soaked and dripping blood. As the days went on, Charlotte's letters would always say, *"And it came to pass."* Her letters always drew me closer to God. She would always have verses for me to read.

As the days, weeks, and months went by, my motivation grew more and more. I was becoming one motivated Marine; pain was no more a deterrent but a motivation. The Drill Instructors tried to get me to sing their dirty songs; I would not. So they would thrash me and send me to the pit, I was punished so many times that I began looking forward to the pit. God blessed me for standing up; I was the only recruit that chose to go to church on Sundays. That was washday, it was when we had to wash and clean our uniform. So by going to church I never got to wash my uniform. But through the disbelief of the Drill Instructors my uniforms were always clean.

"But Jesus beheld *them,* and said unto them, With men this is impossible; but with God all things are possible."

Matthew 19:26

As graduation came closer there were only 40 of us left; I could see that light at the end of the tunnel. All those months there felt like a life time; those 4 months felt like I was born there and at times, I thought I was going to die there. We still had some hard weeks to go. They kept telling us that they were not going to let any of us graduate, more of their mind games. They played mind games such as not giving our letters to us when they arrived, waiting up to three to four weeks to give them to us. They told us our wives had found someone else to love. I saw a lot of guys break during this time, but not me. I knew without a doubt that Charlotte would never leave me.

> "Nevertheless let every one of you in particular so love his wife even as himself; and the wife *see* that she reverence *her* husband."
>
> **Ephesians 5:33**

Charlotte's faithfulness was like Sarah's faithfulness to Abraham.

> "While they behold your chaste conversation *coupled* with fear. Whose adorning let it not be that outward *adorning* of plaiting the hair, and of wearing of gold, or of putting on of apparel; But *let it be* the hidden man of the heart, in that which is not corruptible, *even the ornament* of a meek and quiet spirit, which is in the sight of God of great price. For after this manner in the old time the holy women also,

who trusted in God, adorned themselves, being in subjection unto their own husbands: Even as Sara obeyed Abraham, calling him lord: whose daughters ye are, as long as ye do well, and are not afraid with any amazement."

1 Peter 3:2-6

So their mind games did not work on me.

Back home Charlotte was overcoming her fears. She was becoming a bolder Christian, not just relying on me to do the talking when we went out on visitation.

"And for me, that utterance may be given unto me, that I may open my mouth boldly, to make known the mystery of the gospel,"

Ephesians 6:19

Now she was not scared to tell someone how to know Jesus Christ, the way she knows Him. She was becoming even a stronger and more complete Christian. And the weakness of fear that held her back for so many years was gone. Charlotte had all of her armor on and was ready for battle.

Boot camp was coming to a close; we had just a few days left. Charlotte was flying out to see me graduate. My spirits were high and I could not wait to see Charlotte. By now there were just 36 out of 80 of us that started, that would graduate and be called Marines. But something else was happening to me those last few days. I tried so hard to become a Marine. I thought that Marines made men, but I was wrong. God makes men, the missing piece of the puzzle was not here on earth, but it was my walk with God, a closer relationship with Christ. Just as Charlotte found her missing piece of the puzzle, so had I.

I graduated from boot camp and earned the title Marine. Charlotte and I both have new titles too, "Soldiers for Christ."

> "Thou therefore endure hardness, as a good soldier of Jesus Christ. No man that warreth entangleth himself with the affairs of *this* life; that he may please him who hath chosen him to be a soldier."
>
> **2 Timothy 2:3-4**

The story does not stop here. Both Charlotte and I were ready for battle. I had one week of liberty before I started my school. Our Pastor, Bro. Cavin Meeds, sent 500 tracts with Charlotte to be handed out during our time together. That was the beginning of our tract ministry. So off we went handing out 500 tracts in California. Side by side, two soldiers for Christ, showing people the way to heaven. That week went by so fast. It was time for Charlotte to leave. We hugged and kissed each other good bye knowing that in three months we would be together again. The week I spent with her made me realize that I am the wealthiest man in the world. I have Christ and he gave me Charlotte.

> "Who can find a virtuous woman? for her price *is* far above rubies. The heart of her husband doth safely trust in her, so that he shall have no need of spoil. She will do him good and not evil all the days of her life... Her husband is known in the gates, when he sitteth among the elders of the land... Strength and honour *are* her clothing; and she shall rejoice in time to come. She openeth her mouth with wisdom; and in her tongue *is* the law of kindness. She looketh well to the ways of her household, and eateth not the bread of idleness. Her children arise up, and call her blessed; her husband *also*, and he praiseth her.
>
> **Proverbs 31:10-12, 23, 25-28**

God began to bless me so much, I was appointed fourth squad leader. My goal for the next three months was to tell them about Christ. To a Marine you better walk the walk and talk the talk, if you were going to be a witness for Christ. Training again was hard; many nights were in a tent and training in the field. One night, storm clouds moved in, and it rained so hard that training stopped for the night. So we ran to our tents, two Marines to a tent. As I was laying there I thought that here is an opportunity to tell him about Christ, he is not going anywhere. So I let him have it, with both barrels. I unloaded on him, I preached to him for over an hour. Sad to say he did not except Christ that night. But the next day, we broke camp and marched back to the barracks. We were given the day off to get our gear cleaned up and be ready the next day. I was sitting on my rack when one of my guys walked up to me and said, *"I want Christ as my Saviour."* We knelt down and I led him to the Lord! I asked him what brought him to that decision to follow Christ. He said last night in his tent, he listened to me preach for over an hour. We laughed; I had forgotten how thin the walls of the tent were. I had no idea that his tent was that close to mine. But, Thank God for thin walls.

That day I ran down to main side and called Charlotte to tell her about my first soul I led to the Lord. The phone rang and she picked up and started telling me about this young lady that she led to the Lord, her first. Then I told her about my first soul. We were both rejoicing about how our lives had changed. And now, fighting the fight.

> "I have fought a good fight, I have finished *my* course, I have kept the faith:"
>
> **2 Timothy 4:7**

I asked her what day and time this happened, when she said Saturday around 10:30 am; I was shocked, that was around the time when I led this Marine to the Lord. What a blessing! The next day another Marine came up to me wanting to be saved, so we knelt down and I led him to the Lord. I asked, him "Where did you hear about Christ." He said the same thing, he heard me through the tent walls. Then about a week later another Marine came up to me asking to be saved. So we knelt beside my rack and he asked Jesus into his heart. I asked him what was going on, he said that he wanted what Carillo has. That was the first Marine that got saved. Carillo was from a very rough neighborhood and a member of a gang. He joined to stay out of jail. When I first met Carillo, he was in love with that singer in the 80's named Blondie. He told me that he wanted to marry a girl just like her. I told him, "Not me, I have the perfect wife."

I began to tell him stories about Charlotte. How she was faithful, loves God, and how I was number two in her life. I told him how we met and fell in love, and were serving God together. I told him that no matter how far apart we were, she would always wait for me to come home. If I lost both my legs, she would never leave me. I would read some of my letters to him from Charlotte. After he got saved, he became a new man.

> "Therefore if any man *be* in Christ, *he is* a new creature: old things are passed away; behold, all things are become new."

2 Corinthians 5:17

He even came up to me the day before I was being shipped out and told me that he wanted to marry someone like Charlotte. I said what happened to marrying Blondie. He said, *"You mean that tramp?"* We both laughed and shook hands and hugged and said our goodbyes.

God blessed so much in boot camp and school. I received very high honors. I received meritorious mast and meritorious promotion. And at my next duty station, I became the new com-chief and in less than two years, promoted to platoon Sgt. But what meant the most to me was knowing that I would see those Marines in heaven one day. And that Charlotte and I were a part of it.

"For whosoever shall call upon the name of the Lord shall be saved. How then shall they call on him in whom they have not believed? and how shall they believe in him of whom they have not heard? and how shall they hear without a preacher? And how shall they preach, except they be sent? as it is written, How beautiful are the feet of them that preach the gospel of peace, and bring glad tidings of good things! But they have not all obeyed the gospel. For Esaias saith, Lord, who hath believed our report? So then faith *cometh* by hearing, and hearing by the word of God."

Romans 10:13-17

five

MICHAELS'S MESSAGE

-- 1987-1990 --

L ittle did we know that God was preparing our life for what was about to come. Charlotte's Step-mom gave her a book called Angel Unaware. At night, Charlotte would read page by page to me, and we could not understand how anybody could go through what they went through. Their story starts out like this:

"Our baby came into the world with an appalling handicap, as you will discover when you read her story. I believe with all my heart that God sent her on a two-year mission to our household, to strengthen us spiritually and to draw us closer together in the knowledge and love and fellowship of God. It has been said that tragedy and sorrow never leave us where they find us. In this instance, both Roy and I are grateful to God for the privilege of learning some great lessons of truth through His tiny messenger."

Dale Evans Rogers
August 24, 1952

"Be not forgetful to entertain strangers: for thereby some have entertained angels unawares."

Hebrews 13:2

Their story became our story and the angel that visited them, visited us. And our lives have never been the same. Our story starts out like this…

January 1990
"Michael is dying."
The doctors said it that plain and simple.

Michael, our 2-year old adopted son was dying. That's what they had told us every day during the first week at the hospital. For two days, Michael's temperature was just 92 degrees. His platelet count that was supposed to be 150,000 was down to 4,000. His resistance to disease was virtually gone. He caught pneumonia in one lung, then in the other. He soon developed what the doctors called "white-out" — 100 percent pneumonia — in both lungs.

They needed to do a bone marrow test to see just how far gone his immune system was. But there were problems with conducting the test. Boring through flesh and bone to extract a bone marrow sample is an excruciatingly painful procedure. But the doctors couldn't risk giving Michael any pain-killer other than superficial local anesthetic for the fear that the medication would overtax his already weakened heart and kill him. With general anesthesia, however, the doctors feared that the pain of the bone marrow extraction would kill him.

The dilemma was a serious one for the doctors. It was far less so for us. *"Michael's life is in God's hands,"* we told them. *"If God wants Michael, then he will take him home. If not, then God will allow Michael to live."*

It was not the first time our faith in God and our conviction that the Creator had put Michael on this earth for a purpose had surprised the medical folks. And it was not the first time that, that faith and conviction had been confirmed.

-- 1987 --

Ever since my wife, Charlotte, and I were married in the fall of 1974, we had wanted a child. We were starved for a child. After 10 years of trying, however, it became obvious that we would not be able to fulfill our desire to have children. Adoption seemed the obvious way to fulfill our desire.

Our dreams of a family were dampened after exposure to the realities of adoption – the tremendous expense ($10,000 to $25,000), the long waiting lists. It seemed that realizing our hopes of having a child were still more years in the future.

But then another path was about to open up for us that would lead us on a journey of love, excitement and fulfillment, tempered with disappointment, pain and tears.

The journey began when a friend told us a 14 year old girl was pregnant and wanted a loving couple to care for her baby as if it were their own. When our lawyer contacted her, she was four months pregnant. Her doctor had assured her that the pregnancy was going well and that the baby was doing fine.

The legal arrangements were made and our joy was insurmountable. For the first time in 13 years of our marriage; we were going to be a family.

Later that month, we were at home packing for a vacation to California when the phone rang. It was our lawyer.

"Richard, I've got some bad news for ya'll. The baby's biological father has decided that his sister will take the baby."

It was as if a bomb had exploded in my guts. I don't even remember saying goodbye before I hung up the phone.

As I put the phone down I heard a horn honk outside. It was my parents, ready to take us to the airport. I didn't tell them about the phone call and wasn't going to tell Charlotte until after the vacation, but on the plane she began asking questions about the phone call. *"Who called? What was wrong?"*

I would have rather cut off my arms than to have to tell Charlotte that we were not going to get the baby.

We had long known that the Lord was in charge of our lives and so we knew that there must be a purpose for this happening to us, but the pain was still there. It came along as an uninvited and unwelcome guest on our vacation.

We stayed busy every day of the vacation, going a lot of places, doing a lot of things, but today neither of us remembers much at all about that vacation.

Waiting for us back home was the joyless task of telling our family and friends that we were not going to get the baby. That done, we tried our best to pick up the pieces and go on, but every minute we could think of little else but our baby.

Then one day we received another call from our lawyer, she asked us if we still wanted the baby.

"Yes!" I screamed into the phone. *"Yes, Yes!"*

No one knew why for sure, but the father's sister did not want to adopt the baby. The biological mother wanted to know if we still wanted the child.

I hung up the phone, ran into the bedroom where Charlotte was cleaning and lifted her off the floor and told her the news. We knelt down beside the bed and cried and prayed and thanked God.

By then the biological mother was seven months pregnant. We were making lots of trips back and forth to the lawyer's office to sign papers. Each time, Charlotte, my little detective, would pick up bits of information that finally began falling together like pieces of a puzzle. She put those pieces together and began coming up with a picture of who the biological mother was and where she lived.

Charlotte would don her sunglasses and hat and stake out the lawyer's office. She spotted a girl she believed to be the biological mother and wrote down the license number and description of the car.

Then Charlotte discovered the girl's doctor's name. At this point, I was home from work with a dislocated shoulder and wound up getting drafted into Charlotte's *"Remington Steele"* operation. We staked out the doctor's office and finally saw the girl walk into the office with her father.

When she came back out, we immediately knew something was wrong. She was crying and her dad had to hold her up as they walked to the car.

As we got to our front door the phone was ringing. It was our lawyer. She had some bad news about the baby's health. Could we come over to her office right away?

Bad news was an understatement. The doctor's report on the fetus indicated that the baby had no brain, no bowels and a cleft palate. The doctor said that it would be a miracle if the baby lived to term. If it were born alive it would be another miracle. Right then and there our lawyer, a good Christian who was trying to save us from the pain she saw was coming, advised us to walk away from the whole ordeal. In tears, we told her we would pray before making our decision.

The tears led to prayers. We knew our lives and the baby's life were in the Lord's hands. We called our lawyer and told her that we would trust in the Lord and accept our baby no matter what happened.

We asked that another doctor examine the mother but the test results simply confirmed the first doctor's opinion. Still, we continued to pray.

At the end of the eighth month of her pregnancy, she went into labor. There were complications with the delivery but on August 21, 1987, she gave birth to a baby boy named Michael.

A meeting was set for that night at the hospital.

When we arrived, our lawyer, the doctor and the delivery nurse met us in a small room and told us that it would be best if we went back home and didn't even look at the baby. The doctor told us that Michael could not see or hear and that he had no brain and wouldn't respond to any type of cuddling. He had many other small deformities and we wouldn't be able to console him and it would be a miracle if he lived for more than a month.

We told them, *"We want to see our baby!"*

They took us to the neo-natal nursery where the 5 pound baby was in his incubator, hooked up to an oxygen supply. The nurses took him out and my wife held this little, white- haired baby and he looked cuter than all other "Preemies" around. The doctor had already told me that if the child lived to be 18 years old he would cost us over a million dollars. The doctor said, *"Just turn around and walk off, the child is dying; don't get attached."*

Looking down at the baby I remembered a time five years before when a plant we had in the bathroom was dying. All the leaves were falling off. I told Charlotte to throw it way. She looked up at me with a look that said, *"Please don't make me give up."* There was a little green at the bottom of the stalk and she pointed to it as proof that the plant was still alive.

I looked up from the child that was in Charlotte's arms and into Charlotte's eyes and knew that if we had to live in a tent to be able to afford Michael that we would.

I told the doctors that we might not be able to buy all the things Michael would need, but there was one thing we could afford and that was love.

Before my eyes, Charlotte had become a mother cherishing her child. I knew Michael was going to be a part of us no matter what. We were a family!

-- *1976* --

Once when I was working at a number of odd jobs; I was night manager at a gas station in Amarillo, Texas. Each night, Charlotte would drive to the station in our pickup. I would make a bed for her in the bed of the truck and drive the truck into the gas station garage. Then I'd unplug the bell that rang when a customer pulled into the station so that the noise of the bell wouldn't wake her. Knowing that we were together, that Charlotte was there, even though she was asleep, gave me a feeling of peace. But there was something always missing in our life, a child.

-- *1987* --

Later that night they did some tests because his heart was irregular and his blood count was extremely low at the time of his delivery. The results of those test constituted our first Michael's miracle.

By the time the test was completed, Michael's heart rate and blood count were normal.

The doctor turned to us and said that the only thing that could explain the turn-around was that

Michael had somehow sensed that someone wanted and needed him. Michael had felt loved.

On top of those test results, the doctors told us that Michael did have a small brain, after all, that his bowels were normal, he didn't have a cleft palate and that he could hear. He also said that he did seem to love to be cuddled.

The nurses named him the "Cabbage Patch Kid" because he really did look just like a "Preemie" in the Cabbage Patch series.

We soon brought Michael home. He was a good baby. He slept well and ate reasonably well, although there were times during the first few months when Charlotte hardly slept in our bedroom because Michael had an unusually sensitive gag reflex. It took him two to three hours to drink a bottle. But Charlotte never grew weary of daily tasks.

Michael grew stronger and we began to see signs of improvement. He was beginning to smile and giggle and was even trying to crawl at times. In fact, the therapist said that his development was normal at four months.

Then the nightmares began.

We were at my parents' house and Charlotte had just finished feeding Michael. She was in the kitchen and I was in the living room when I heard Charlotte scream.

I ran into the kitchen, where Charlotte was holding Michael in her arms. He was quivering all over. He obviously could not breathe. His face turned blue and his small body went limp.

After about two minutes that seemed like an eternity, we heard Michael take a deep breath. Life began to seep back into his face.

When we talked to the doctor he told us that this was going to be an every day occurrence, because of the small size of Michael's brain.

As the days went on, the seizures got worse, until Michael was averaging 13 grand mal seizures a day. The neurologist told us that the drugs, Michael's mother or father had taken may have lain dormant in their systems but, in effect, come to life when Michael was conceived and that the drugs had caused multiple defects and damaged his brain.

As an electrical power overload can cause short circuits, Michael's seizures were caused by an overload of input, with no place for the input to go, no place for it to be stored.

The doctor said that any kind of drug, even marijuana, could create a chemical imbalance in the body for years, like some monster hiding in the shadows. When the person who uses the drugs decides to become a mother or father, the monster can leap out of hiding and wreak havoc not just in the drug user's life but in the life of the unborn child. Michael was a casualty, a victim of the monster's wrath. He paid the price for his parent's few moments of highs with a lifetime of lows.

As the seizures got more violent, we had to try to hold Michael down once. I would lay on his little arms and Charlotte would lay on his little legs and the seizures were so hard that they would lift Charlotte off the ground and I was unable to hold his arms still.

As I lay on the living room floor with Michael crying and screaming, I noticed Charlotte was crying too. Tears welled up in my eyes. With my whole family in tears, I thought about what a terrible price Michael was being forced to pay.

An ophthalmologist's examination would bring more bad news. We had been told that there might be some hope for Michael's vision once the cataracts were removed. But the ophthalmologist found that the optic nerve was faded, Michael's retinas scarred. The cataracts were the least of his problems. The doctor said he didn't know exactly what had caused all the damage to Michael's eyes but he said it was as if battery acid had begun to scar the eyes from the inside out.

The old monster had struck again.

The ophthalmologist said that in any case, Michael had gone through some painful development during the pregnancy. I can't imagine how Michael might have felt or what he was going through as his eyes were being destroyed, burned from the inside.

Did he scream inside the womb, begging for the hurt to stop? The hurt didn't stop, though, until the monster had done his work.

Michael began to retreat into a shell. From time to time a look of terror would shadow his face because the monster was coming back, pulling him into a jerking, shuddering seizure.

His development regressed to the point that smiling, laughing and trying to crawl were merely memories. The doctors told us now that Michael will never progress past the four month old level, all because of the genetic damage inflicted by the drugs his parents used.

-- January 1990 --

The monster was back that week in the hospital, not long ago, when Michael was battling pneumonia. He won that battle, with God's help, just as he has been winning battles with that kind of help for his lengthy short life.

About 10 people were in the room at the hospital when the bone marrow extraction procedure began. Charlotte held Michael's head in her lap and two nurses held Michael's legs. Because of Michael's weakened state, they could not give him anything for the pain except local anesthetic.

The doctor started to drill into the bone and I could hear Charlotte quoting the 23rd Psalm:

"The LORD *is* my shepherd; I shall not want. He maketh me to lie down in green pastures: he leadeth me beside the still waters. He restoreth my soul: he leadeth me in the paths of righteousness for his name's sake. Yea, though I walk through the valley of the shadow of death, I will fear no evil: for thou *art* with me; thy rod and thy staff they comfort me. Thou preparest a table before me in the presence of mine enemies: thou anointest my head with oil; my cup runneth over. Surely goodness and mercy shall follow me all the days of my life: and I will dwell in the house of the LORD for ever."

Michael did not kick, scream, cry or move. The doctor couldn't believe it. After the procedure, Michael grew stronger and stronger and was ready to go home in another week. Before he left, he was the talk of the hospital. Once again, Michael proved more of a witness for God than many Christians who can walk, talk, and see.

When people see Michael and they hear about his problems and all the difficulties we face in raising him, they ask us, "What will Michael ever be able to do?"

We answer, that he can do nothing and yet he can do everything. He cannot walk, but through his suffering he can carry a message to the world of the horrors of drug abuse. He cannot see but he can help others see the risks parents can force upon their unborn children. He cannot talk but he can empower a strong voice inside each one of us, especially young people, when tempted with destructive behavior, such as drugs, profanity, alcohol abuse, sexual promiscuity.

Then Michael's voice can speak loudly and be heard clearly enough: *"When in doubt,"* Michael says, *"Don't!"*

Michael Ashford went home to be with the Lord on December 7, 1990. Even in his death God proved yet again his great loving kindness and tender mercies to the Ashford Family.

Charlotte and Richard Ashford awaited the birth of the second child they were to adopt who was due December 15th. In God's perfect timing, Angela Dawn was born early and healthy on December 3rd. Two days later she left the hospital and arrived at her special new home to meet big brother Michael.

As he napped that Friday afternoon, Michael

passed away peacefully without the seizures that were everyday occurrences throughout his short life. Charlotte's efforts at CPR were fruitless this time; Michael's life on this earth was over and now he was being ushered into a far greater place where pain, blindness and lame limbs were not allowed.

The Ashford's do praise God for the gift of Michael. The Lord knew in all his great wisdom just who to let take care of little Michael, for they loved this special child with a deep, unselfish love. How fortunate for Michael Ashford to have such parents as you, Richard and Charlotte Ashford. God bless you and God bless Angela Dawn, who was so lovingly, graciously and perfectly placed in your tender care. By Sheila Long.

six

CHILD PROTECTIVE
SERVICES (CPS)

-- *March 1990* --

As we travel back about 9 months in time, before Angela was born and before Michael passed away, Charlotte was getting the routine down on feeding Michael and taking care of all his needs. Charlotte and I still wanted to adopt one more child. We heard that CPS was looking for parents to adopt their children. They were kids that were abused or neglected; the courts in most cases had to take away the children from those parents because the children were in danger.

When we called, they said that they have to come into the home several times to do a home study and a background check. Then we would go through some classes. We knew we had nothing to hide, a strong marriage and beautiful home. I was working at Pantex for about 5 years. I had a good income and good insurance.

They did their background check and we passed with flying colors. This lady (Barbara) worked for

CPS and was assigned to us for our home study. Everything was going great. We started our classes. Things could not have looked better. We were told that we rated high on the list. We filled out a form on what our preferences would be. We said it does not matter what race or age the child is; we would love to have a baby or a young toddler would be ideal. But we would take any age child.

After she reviewed our files, she began to tell us some of the kids that would fit perfect in our home. We began to get our hopes up. We still had about another 2 to 3 weeks of classes left and one more home study. We were told that we were on the top of the list. With our hopes up, we started to build on another couple of rooms. So just in case there were siblings that needed a home, we would have plenty of room.

There was nothing stopping us on adding to our family. We were praying and our church was praying too. Barbara became our friend, we thought.

We were in the middle of our revival, that week of class. Charlotte and I thought it would be nice to invite our new friend to the revival I walked up to Barbara, with Charlotte beside me, and began to tell her of this great revival we were having and it would be an honor if she would come as our honored guest. We told her how the church was praying for her and us. The smile that she always had on her face, the laughter in her eyes, suddenly was gone. She became stone cold. We both felt the same chill run straight through us.

It was as if our new friend died. And we were standing for the first time in front of a stranger. You could feel the coldness in her voice, when she said, "No thanks." That was when we looked at each other and thought at the same time, "She's lost, she needs Christ with her. And began to pray that someday soon she would accept Him into her heart.

One day during class we had a 15 minute break. We got up and started handing out tracts to everybody. Charlotte even handed one to Barbara. We knew things were going downhill fast, when she walked over to the trash and threw the tract into it. But we still thought that we were going to adopt a child. We thought that we probably were not on the top of the list anymore. But we were just happy to be on the list.

All we had was one more home study. By now the other two rooms were just about finished. When Barbara came out to do the last home study, the days of talking and laughing were gone. She was there for business and that was all. She started telling us that we failed the home study and were not fit to be parents. It caught us off guard; we never saw that punch coming. We were in complete shock!

I turned to look at Charlotte, tears were rolling

down her face. I have seen Charlotte spend count-
less hours feeding and taking care of Michael. I
have woke up at 3 A.M. wondering where she was,
I would find her taking care of Michael all night
long, not even making it to bed and never once did
she ever complain. And here is this woman telling
my wife that she is an unfit mother. I was so mad. I
asked Barbara what she meant that we were are unfit
parents. Her exact words were, *"I would rather have a
lesbian couple raise her children, than a Christian couple."* I escorted her out the door, and when I walked
back into the room, Charlotte was crying. Up until
that day I never saw Charlotte cry so hard. I tried to
console her, but the hurt was too deep. That's when
her nightmares began. In her sleep she would hear
those words, *"That she was an unfit mother,"* time
and time again. She would toss and turn all night
long; she tried not to let me hear her cry. But each
night as I lay my head down, I could hear her crying
in her pillow.

I felt so helpless, I knew God was in control,
but still it was hard to let go of the pain. I wanted to
make it right for Charlotte, but I could not.

I even told her that I am praying for Barbara's
head to explode. I saw Charlotte's smile just a little. I
told Charlotte that during the 1000 year reign, that
God was going to put Barbara under her rule. And
she would have 1000 years of payback.

I told Charlotte we were not giving up. The next day we hired this Christian lawyer. The battle was on; we were going to fight her ruling. Our lawyer requested arbitration. They set up our day in court. The church was praying; all of our friends and all of our kin folk were praying too. We were ready for a battle.

As we walked in their little court room, we saw the panel of people to our right and Barbara and her representative to our left. Little did we know that we were going head to head with Satan and his angels. We thought we were going to put Barbara on trial, but it turned out that we were on trial. And we were the guilty ones, fighting for our life.

I told them what Barbara said about not wanting a Christian couple to raise her children, but rather a lesbian couple to raise them. You can guess what she said next, she denied it all. Barbara said that we both misunderstood her.

But then she asked us this one question that destroys any hope for us getting to adopt through CPS. Her one question was, *"Do you believe the Bible?"*

I said, *"Yes, of course we do."*

Then she asked, *"Do you believe it is the Word of God?"*

I said, *"Yes!"*

"If the Bible said to do something, would you do it or not?"

"Yes we will do what God tells us to do."

Then she said if CPS said you will not do something and the Bible said to do it, what would you do? I said I would do what the Bible told me to do! Barbara went over to the desk and picked up the Bible and read from Proverbs 22:15.

> "Foolishness *is* bound in the heart of a child; *but* the rod of correction shall drive it far from him."
>
> **Proverbs 22:15**

She turned to us and said, *"You know our rules; you will never spank our children. CPS will not allow you to abuse our children, and beat them, so Richard and Charlotte, are you going to do what we say or what this Bible says?"* That's when she took the Bible she was holding and slammed it down on the table.

I stood up and said, *"We are going to do what God's word says to do. But you people need to know the difference between discipline and abuse. Discipline is done out of love, abuse is done out of hate. There is such a big difference, between the two."*

Everything I said was falling on deaf ears; I said my peace and sat down. They left for about 10 minutes and then walked back and sat down. One of the board members stood up and stated that they will not overturn Barbara's decision. We were deemed unfit parents. We lost again!

Charlotte's shoulders began to slump and the tears began to flow again. Satan had struck again, and all seemed hopeless.

Charlotte began to pray that just because one door closed that another door be open. I was still praying for Barbara's head to explode.

God heard Charlotte's prayers. And as you know by now, my prayers, were not answered. Barbara's head never went up in flames or exploded.

> "Be careful for nothing; but in everything by prayer and supplication with thanksgiving let your requests be made known unto God."
> **Philippians 4:6**

That day at work I was so mad and angry and felt helpless. All I could do was gripe about how they have hurt us and left my wife in tears. Everybody that I saw that day knew I was angry, so when I walked into a room, everybody would leave. All except one lady, Linda. She asked me what was wrong. So I told her everything and she listened,

When I was through griping, Linda said, "I know you and Charlotte, you two are not unfit parents - The love, and dedication and unselfishness that you have shown raising a handicap boy. They are so stupid not allowing you two a chance on giving some child a loving home. Then Linda began to tell me about this girl that was going to give up her unborn child. They were sending the final papers up to be signed and finalized. But this girl wanted to meet the adoptive parents. But their lawyer said, "no way." She knew that with her little boy, she had her hands full and could not raise a newborn baby and a little boy. So that next day she was going to agree with their terms and sign the papers.

Linda said, "I know this girl; she is my daughter's best friend. It is a shot in the dark, and don't get your hopes up. I will talk to her and tell her to hold off signing the papers." Then Linda said, "Are you sure you want to get Charlotte's hopes up again? This girl could change her mind, and at the last moment, not give her baby up for adoption."

I said we can't give up trying. I went home that night and told Charlotte about this pregnant girl that Linda knows. I said, "Charlotte don't get your hopes up."

Charlotte is a warrior, she never gives up. She looked up at me with Michael in her arms, and said "Let's pray and go for it." She said, "It is all in God's hands.

"…for he hath said, I will never leave thee, nor forsake thee."

Hebrews 13:5

I called Linda up the next day and asked her what the girl said. Linda said that she will hold off signing the papers but she wanted to meet us. I told Linda that was ok with us. The next day we were introduced to Betty, who by then, was about 4 months pregnant. When we met Betty, we fell in love with her and her little boy, Derek. It was not long after that meeting that Betty said she wanted us to be the adoptive parents to the baby. The tears that ran down Charlotte's face last week began to run down her face again. But this time it was not the tear of sadness or sorrows, they were tears of happiness, joy and peace.

"They that sow in tears shall reap in joy."
Psalms 126:5

Everything went as planned and a beautiful baby girl that we named Angela was born on December 3, 1990. And as you have read Michael's story; he went home to be with our Lord and Saviour on December 7, 1990. God's perfect timing. God took Michael home and gave us Angela. God always comes through.

As the years went by, we lost contact with Betty (Angela's birth mom). We sent pictures of Angela to Betty, but a lot of them came back, address unknown. Betty was going through some dark and hard times, in and out of jail and in and out of relationships ,too. Angela wanted to meet her big bother. She was 5 years old and Derek was 10 years old. We thought that it might help Betty to see how well Angela was doing; and it did for a little while. We all met at the park and Angela and Derek hit it off. Angela asked Derek if he wanted to go to Church with her. He said yes! And that turned out to be one of the best things that ever happened to him. That week Derek asked Jesus Christ into his heart. Things were looking up for him; he loved being with Angela and coming to Church. But then Satan never sits still; Derek's dad would not let him come to Church anymore. And that's when Satan stepped in and began to destroy Derek's life. He first began to run with the wrong kind of friends. He started smoking and drinking. Then he got into drugs. Then spent some time in jail. His life began to turn out just like his mom's. Soon his life was out of control. And 10 years later when he turned 20 years old. Derek bought some drugs at a teenage hang out. Those drugs were bad, he started to get sick and someone called an ambulance. He never made it to the hospital, DOA.

The story you read next is Charlotte's, Our Silent Warrior speaks out. The Holy Spirit moved in Charlotte's heart and this is her message: "I read in the newspaper that the funeral was in a few days and that it was going to be at a Mormon church but no preacher was going to speak. So the Lord kept waking me up in the middle of the night to let me know what I was going to say. I'm not a speaker or a good talker in front of crowds but the Lord was preparing me to speak at the funeral. Each night I would wake up and practice the same words and scriptures."

"The day of Derek's funeral came and Angela and I went by ourselves because Richard had to work. The Lord had a hand in that because I would have let Richard speak if he was there. The Lord gave me a peace. "

> "And the peace of God, which passeth all understanding, shall keep your hearts and minds through Christ Jesus."
>
> **Philippians 4:7**

"As we sat down in the church I would see around 200 people there, from bikers to skateboarders to drug addicts; and all of Betty's family which are mostly Christians and they got to hear for the first time that Derek was Saved. "

"I was the first to speak after Betty's brother Mike prayed. I was not scared in the least bit and the Holy Spirit spoke right through me. I took the microphone and told them how Angela was 5 and Derek was 10 when they met at a park. Angela was so proud of having a new brother that she invited him to church.

"Richard had a Sunday School class for ten year old boys and was teaching about heaven that day and Derek listened to every word. Richard said that in Heaven there would be no sorrow, pain or sickness, After class ,Derek went up to Richard and said that he wanted to know how he could go to Heaven. So Richard opened his Bible to Romans 3:23 and read,

"For all have sinned, and come short of the glory of God;"

"And Richard asked Derek if he knew that sin is the bad things we do and if knew he was a sinner and Derek said that he was a sinner! And Richard read John 3:16, "

"For God so loved the world, that he gave his only begotten Son, that whosoever believeth in him should not perish, but have everlasting life."

"And that life is in heaven. And he read Romans 5:8, "

"But God commendeth [or showed]his love toward us, in that, while we were yet sinners, Christ died for us."

"And we can go to Heaven if we repent and accept him as our Saviour. Romans 10:9 and 13 says,

"That if thou shalt confess with thy mouth the Lord Jesus, and shalt believe in thine heart that God hath raised him from the dead, thou shalt be saved ... For whosoever shall call upon the name of the Lord shall be saved."

"And if you pray to him and ask him to save you he will. So Derek prayed, *"I know I'm a sinner, please forgive me of my sins and come into my heart and save me and take me to heaven when I die."*

Then I said, *"If there are any of you here today that have not accepted the Lord as your Saviour, if Derek was here today he would want all of you to repent and accept him today so you, too, can go to heaven. And be with Derek one day!"*

Then Charlotte stepped down and after the service was over, Charlotte and Angela handed out over 200 tracts. God's word was heard that day and many seeds were planted. As for Betty, in the days following Derek's homegoing, her world grew more and more dark. The world that was her comfort, was now her nightmare. The men that were in her life, came and went. The promises that Satan has told her now were just lies. Betty has been through and has caused so much pain for her loved ones. The fun and freedom that she desired as a teenager is now her bondage. Betty is a Slave unto Sin!

"Let not sin therefore reign in your mortal body, that ye should obey it in the lusts thereof."

Romans 6:12

But through her loved ones, we are praying for her return.

"Pray without ceasing."

1 Thessalonians 5:17

seven

Our Home Became a Tent

-- 1994 --

Our little church we were going to, needed a pastor. Some of the Deacons came up to me and asked me to call this retired Pastor, Dr. M.O. Garner, and see if he would come up and help us out. I called him up that night and told him that we could not pay much, "but will you come and help us out?" He said yes, and for over the next two years, he helped us get back on our feet. The church began to be blessed and began to grow again. We became close friends, and he taught me how a pastor should lead his flock. He was a great mentor and friend to me.

One day he came up to me and asked if I would go into building houses with him. I always liked learning a new trade. He said when he retired in California that what he was doing was building houses. So day by day he showed me what to do and how to handle each problem that came up. Our first house became our last house together. His health became bad, the stress and work became too hard, so he asked me to take the business over and run with it. So off I ventured on my own. I went to every bank to get a construction loan. No one knew me and would not loan me any money. So Charlotte and I and our little daughter got on our knees and prayed.

The next day, this one bank said that they would loan me half of the amount on the first house and if they liked what they saw, they would loan me 100 % from then on. I was so happy. I needed $90,000 on this first house, the bank said that they would loan $45,000 if I came up with $45,000. There was one little problem, I did not have $45,000. As I was driving home and praying, that's when an idea popped into my head. If we would sell everything we had and move into a tent, we could start our adventure. It sounded like a good idea to me. I drove home excited about my idea of selling everything we had. I will never forget the look on Charlotte's face when I told her of my idea. My loving and always trusting wife looked into my eyes and said, "Ok!" WOW! Did I marry the perfect wife; she is as crazy as I am!

And that is what we did, sold it all! And moved into this little Pop-up tent. And started RCA Builders. The RCA stood for Richard, Charlotte and Angela. With our tent we moved to KOA campground. I still worked at Pantex and on our days off we built this first spec house.

The next week my boss called me into his office

and said he just received my notice of a different address. He asked me if this address was right. I looked down at what was written, KOA campground, space #6. I looked up and said, "yes." Then he began to tell me how sorry he was that I was getting a divorce. And that he would have never believed in his lifetime that he'd see Charlotte and me split up. He asked me if he could do anything to get us back together. I said we are not getting a divorce. I told him what we are doing and that we are still a family living in a tent. He could not believe it. My boss asked me three times, "You moved into a tent and sold all you have and Charlotte said ok, and lives in a tent with you?" *"Yes,"* I said, *"And our 3 year old daughter Angela is with us too."* He told me that if he came home and asked his wife to do that, she would divorce him. Three years later they divorced. I always wondered if he asked her to move into a tent.

Back to building houses, Charlotte knew that our goal was to some day build our house and pay cash for it. So side by side we were chasing our dream, God gave me a wife that never has thought of herself; she had always put me and Angela first. I can give her $20.00 and next week when I need $20.00 for something, out pops the $20.00 that I gave her. I even have to make her buy a dress for herself. That's the kind of wife I married!

Back in the tent, the nights were getting colder

and colder, Fall had come and gone. Winter was just around the corner. The girls loved it. I was freezing to death; I have never been so cold in my life. I would get up at 3:30 a.m. to get ready for work. It's hard to knock the frost off your face and shave. I would look back at Charlotte; she would always have a smile. Her smile would always warm up my heart. Knowing that I have Charlotte by my side makes me feel like a winner. No money in the world can buy the happiness that I have. But it came at a price, and that price was when God sent his Son to die in our place.

> "For God so loved the world, that he gave his only begotten Son, that whosoever believeth in him should not perish, but have everlasting life."
>
> **John 3:16**

We lived in that tent for about 4 months; at night the temperature would drop down in the 20's and 30's. Then we sold our first house. God blessed and we started putting that money aside for our new house some day.

One Sunday, one of our friends said that they had an old trailer we could use, more of God's blessings. He said the heater does not work but if we wanted to use it, we are welcome to it, so he pulled it up to the KOA campground and we moved in it. We all were so happy; you would have thought that we were moving into a million dollar home. God has taught Charlotte to be happy and count her blessings, so for the next six months we lived in this beat up trailer. The heater did not work, bathroom did not work, hot water heater did not work, and most of the lights did not work. But it was our home and we loved it, and the building was going strong. And from then on, we sold all of our houses before they were finished. Charlotte painted, scraped, sanded, and cleaned, getting all the houses ready for the next stage. As the years went by, we lived in tents, trailers, apartments, and garages. I think we spent two Christmas's in garages. Angela grew up playing with cut up blocks of wood.

As a 4 year old girl, she knew just about everything there was about building a house. One Saturday she woke us up one morning, and she said, *"Daddy get up!"*

I said, *"Honey what's wrong?"*

This little 4 year old girl, and those big beautiful brown eyes, wide open said, *"Its time to get up , we have an electrician to call, painters to get going, and bricker's to get started."* I looked at Charlotte and said if she was just a little bit older, I would let her have this business. We gave Angela a big hug.

I told Charlotte that when she was tired of all this building business, all she had to do was come up to me and tell me she was tired. That day came six years later, when I was making a deal on selling this house we built. She came up and whispered in my ear, *"I'm tired."* I looked at this guy, told him *"I am sorry, I just retired."* I handed him a set of blueprints and recommended another builder. I turned to Charlotte and said,"Is this the house you want?" She said, *"YES!"* I checked my building loan to see what money we needed to finish paying off this loan. The loan was for $190,000. So we went to our savings that we had, since we started building houses. We could not believe it, another of God's blessings. We had in our savings $190,000. Boy, did we rejoice! The dream that we had, had come true. God gave us the desire of our hearts.

> "Delight thyself also in the LORD; and he shall give thee the desires of thine heart. Commit thy way unto the LORD; trust also in him; and he shall bring *it* to pass."
>
> **Psalms 37:4-5**

If you do the desires of God, then God will bless your home. Make his desires your desires and make Christ the most important part of your life.

> "Therefore whosoever heareth these sayings of mine, and doeth them, I will liken him unto a wise man, which built his house upon a rock: And the

rain descended, and the floods came, and the winds blew, and beat upon that house; and it fell not: for it was founded upon a rock. And every one that heareth these sayings of mine, and doeth them not, shall be likened unto a foolish man, which built his house upon the sand: And the rain descended, and the floods came, and the winds blew, and beat upon that house; and it fell: and great was the fall of it.

Matthew 7:24-27

Before you start trying to build your life, make sure your foundation is Jesus Christ.

"THERE IS NO GOD!"

-- 2001-2005 --

God started to burden our hearts to be more of a witness for him. God wanted us to witness to everybody that we met. As usual, Charlotte said, "Let's pray and see how God provides. So we prayed that week and God provided on how to be a witness to everybody we came in contact with. Tracts!! That is how we can get the message out, by handing out tracts on how to become a Christian. But we have done that before and when people see it's a Church Tract, they throw most of them away. So back to the drawing board and keep on praying.

That week Charlotte told me a true story about an atheist and a Preacher. And when she finished the story, I looked at her and said, "That's the story we need to put in our tracts."

We needed something that will draw people into the story and the next thing you know they would be reading how to get Saved. So I started to write and it came flowing out.

That night I went to work to try to finish up the tract and try to come up with the title, something eye catching. And Charlotte was at home praying for God to give me wisdom.

That night, God gave me a name for the title. "THERE IS NO GOD" All night I wrestled against God; I told God that I am not going to put "THERE IS NO GOD" as a title. As I drove home that morning from work, my heart was about to burst. God said Yes! And I said NO! When I drove up into the garage that morning, Charlotte was there waiting for me. She always had a smile and a kiss for me. When she saw my face, Charlotte asked, "What is wrong?" I began to tell her what God wanted as a title for the tract. And I did not want to name it that.

Charlotte looked into my eyes and said, *"Honey, that is a scripture."* I could not believe what I was hearing. Charlotte said, *"It is in Psalms 14:1,*

"The fool hath said in his heart, *There is* no God…"

Wow! What a relief. That took a big burden off me. I told Charlotte that God had us to write a tract that would be disguised and not look like a church tract. If Satan can be a wolf in sheep's clothing, then these tracts can be a sheep in wolves clothing.

That day Angela began typing and getting the right picture for the front of the tract. And Charlotte put it all together with the final touches. The front of the tract has a beautiful picture of mountains and an old gold mining trail leading up toward the top. With Written in the sky is "THERE IS NO GOD" and the story inside goes like this:

THERE IS NO GOD…That's what this big man was saying to this old country preacher, *"There is No God!"* This man began to make fun and argue with this preacher.

The preacher looked this man in the eyes and said, *"Believe on the Lord Jesus Christ and thou shalt be saved."*

That big man began to laugh and mock him, and said, *"I don't see God standing around anywhere, where is he?"*

The preacher said, *"Believe on the Lord Jesus Christ and thou shalt be saved."* This man looked at his friends and they were laughing too!

This big man said, *"If there is a God, have him do some miracle."* That old man of God said, *"Believe on the Lord Jesus Christ and thou shalt be saved."*

The big man said, *"I've committed almost every sin in that Bible of yours."*

The preacher said, *"Believe on the Lord Jesus Christ and thou shalt be saved."*

Then the man said, *"But I love my women and my beer!"*

The preacher said, *"Believe on the Lord Jesus Christ*

and thou shalt be saved." The man began to argue and come up with every reason why there was no GOD! And that old country preacher said. *"Believe on the Lord Jesus Christ and thou shalt be saved."*

The big man went home that night pretty happy that he had made a fool out of that preacher. But as he laid his head down that night ,he tried to sleep.

You guessed it; all he could think about was that preacher's voice saying, *"Believe on the Lord Jesus Christ and thou shalt be saved."*

You see, the word of God is quick, and powerful, and sharper than any two-edged sword and it never comes back void.

He began to toss and turn and get scared. He thought, *"What if there is a God and I am wrong, what if there is a hell and when I die that's where I am going!"* He spent all night long tossing and turning and thinking of the words of the preacher. That next day as soon as the sun came up, that big man ran to the preacher's house, knocked on the door and when the preacher answered, he saw that big man crying. The man asked, *"How can I believe in God? I want to believe in God, the way you do!"* And you guessed it, that old preacher said, *"Believe on the Lord God Jesus Christ and thou shalt be saved."*

You see, it is that simple, yet thousands die daily without Jesus. The Bible says:

"For God so loved the world, that he gave his only begotten Son, that whosoever believeth in him should not perish, but have everlasting life."

John 3:16

"... now is the accepted time; behold, now is the day of salvation ..."

2 Corinthians 6:2

Knowing that Jesus died in your place, for your sins, and is now sitting at the right hand throne of God, is not enough! You must believe in your heart and confess with your mouth that Jesus Christ is Lord of your life and receive him into your heart. God made it that simple!

Please, Pray this Prayer:

Dear God, I believe! I believe that I am a sinner; I believe that your Son, Jesus Christ died for my sins. Please, Jesus come into my heart and forgive me of my sins. I believe and give you my life, my heart and my soul.

In Jesus name,
Amen

"The fool hath said in his heart, *There is* no God ..."

Psalm 14:1

That big man is no fool anymore because he believes on the Lord Jesus Christ.

When Charlotte got the final finishes done we took it to the print shop to see what it would cost for 20,000 tracts. They told us around $1000 dollars. I didn't have that kind of money.

She said that we have that in savings. She also said, *"We can't take it with us when we die."*

"No we can't," I said, *"but I think it's going to kill me writing out the check!"*

The look on Charlotte's face made me feel like everything is going to be ok. God has always taken care of us.

> "Trust in the LORD with all thine heart; and lean not unto thine own understanding. In all thy ways acknowledge him, and he shall direct thy paths.
> **Proverbs 3:5-6**

A week later the tracts were ready. Here are some stories of what happened next.

That next week we were getting ready for vacation, going to Louisiana for family camp. We set a goal to hand out a 1000 tracts.

So the first stop was at Love's Truck Stop. We all took a handful of tracts and off we went, handing out tracts to everybody that looked at us and to some that didn't. Charlotte went up to some girls working behind the Subway counter, and gave them some tracts to read on their break.

As we got our food and were loading up into the car to drive off, a girl was running out to stop us. She asked us, "Are you the ones handing out the tracts?"

My first thoughts were that we were in trouble. I said "Yes, we handed out those tracts. Come to find out, this girl and her best friend work together at Subway. And when Charlotte handed them some tracts, she was trying to tell her friend about God. Her friend told her, just seconds before Charlotte handed them a tract, *"There is no God."*

When her friend looked down at the tract and read "There is No God!" They both ran to the back and dropped to their knees and began to read that tract. She looked at her friend, both crying and there on her knees she accepted Christ as her Lord and Saviour.

> "That if thou shalt confess with thy mouth the Lord Jesus, and shalt believe in thine heart that God hath raised him from the dead, thou shalt be saved. For with the heart man believeth unto righteousness; and with the mouth confession is made unto salvation."
> **Romans 10:9-10**

Wow! That was the first 20 tracts out of a 1000 to be handed out. And we were on fire!

We began putting them on cars and giving them

to anybody walking to their cars. We went into stores and handed tracts out. We even stopped in Fort Worth and picked up our friends and went down-town to hand out more tracts.

There was this one bookstore we all went in and started giving tracts out. Charlotte and I walked by some books that had Hillary Clinton's face on the front.

We looked at each other, not saying a word; a smile was coming on Charlotte's face. Without one word being said, we started putting tracts in all of Hillary Clinton's books. How fitting, "There is No God" tracts in all these books. There must have been at least 30 books of hers. And who said you can't have fun serving God?

The next day we all left for church camp. But before we got there, we stopped at Wal-Mart. The girls had to pick up more lipstick and junk. And Charlotte knows I hate going into the store when they are getting girl junk.

So I stayed outside by the front door handing out tracts.

I looked up and saw a man running toward me, asking me for a tract. As soon as I gave him one, he began walking back to his car, reading the tract. Then a store manager walked out of the store and came over to me. Well, I thought at least I handed out about 15 tracts. But as he walked up to me, he said, "Do you know who that man was you gave a tract to? That man just found out that he has full blown AIDS. And the doctors told him he only has a month to live." This store manager looked at me and said, *"Thank you!"*

The next couple of days at family camp were so good. At camp we laughed, prayed and cried together. That week of family camp and seeing souls saved was a great vacation. Oh! By the way, we handed out over 1000 tracts that week. That week we fulfilled part of the Great Commission that God has called all of us to do!

> "Go ye therefore, and teach all nations, baptizing them in the name of the Father, and of the Son, and of the Holy Ghost: Teaching them to observe all things whatsoever I have commanded you: and, lo, I am with you alway, *even* unto the end of the world. Amen."
>
> **Matthew 28:19-20**

Another time we were at the mall in Amarillo, we were walking up to go inside and there were about 20 teenagers outside, smoking, laughing and talking. So we started handing out tracts, asking them to please read them. We walked inside and I told Charlotte to look back. As we looked back all 20 teenagers were reading the tracts. And for about 5 minutes they were not talking, they were just reading the tracts. And if you know anything at all about teenagers, that was a miracle.

Inside the mall there is the lady that works as a security guard, she is known in many churches as the Tract Nazi.

A friend of ours told Charlotte that she was handing out tracts inside, when the tract Nazi saw her. She went and got another security guard and they arrested her and took her into the back office. This lady began to yell at Charlotte's friend and scare her into never handing out tracts at the mall again. And after what seemed and eternity, they let her go.

Always before when we laid down some church tracts on the benches, she would come by and throw them into the trash. But this time she looked down and saw "There Is No God" tract and left them there. It is so much fun to defeat Satan.

There was this other time we were handing out tracts in the Dallas Mall. Charlotte handed this man a tract while he was walking by. He never stopped walking while he was reading the tract. Charlotte told me to look up and when I did, we watched him run right into a wall. He never stopped reading.

Then there was a time in San Antonio during Fiesta week that this church was handing out tracts. This sweet older Christian lady handed a tract to this man that was drunk and belligerent. He looked down at the tract and wadded it up and threw it at her. Then he looked down at her with a look that scared this lady; she turned and walked off, a little shaken, but ok. But this is where the story had just begun. There was a lady that saw all that went on. She walked up to that crumpled tract, picked it up and unfolded it. Then she sat down on a bench and began reading it. The Holy Spirit began to convict her, and pierce her heart. She bowed her head right there and accepted Christ as her Lord and Saviour.

> "For the word of God *is* quick, and powerful, and sharper than any twoedged sword, piercing even to the dividing asunder of soul and spirit, and of the joints and marrow, and *is* a discerner of the thoughts and intents of the heart."
>
> **Hebrews 4:12**

Charlotte and I were blessed that night in this church in San Antonio, when this lady gave her testimony, that since she accepted Christ, she has not missed one day of church in 10 years.

There are so many more stories of people that accepted Christ through our tract ministry. Our family now has several churches that are handing out our tracts. God has truly blessed the RCA Tract Ministry. One of the only things that Charlotte and I want in life is for Angela to love and serve God and when we walk through those gates of heaven. To hear those words from God,

> "...Well done, *thou* good and faithful servant..."
>
> **Matthew 25:21**

nine

THE PHONE CALL
"THE DEVIL STRIKES AGAIN"

-- 2008 --

The phone rang, and rang and rang again. Charlotte was in the back bedroom and thought she heard the phone. As she opened the bedroom door and ran to the phone, she thought it might be Angela saying that her friend was bringing her home from shopping in a few minutes.

But the voice she heard on the phone was not our daughter; it was one of those phone calls that no parent ever wants to hear!

"Are you Angela's mom?" a lady said,

And Charlotte said, *"What's wrong?"*

She said that Angela had been in a bad wreck! Then my wife asked if she was conscience and where the wreck was. The lady told her at I-40 and Hope Road and Charlotte said that she would be there right away!

I was at work when my pager went off; it was a message to call Charlotte, that there was an emergency! I ran to a phone and called Charlotte's cell phone. When she answered the phone, I could hear sirens going off in the background, people yelling, and a lot of commotion going on. Then I heard Charlotte say, *"Angela has been in a bad wreck, I am in the ambulance with her now and I will meet you at the trauma unit at Northwest Texas Hospital."* Later was when I found out that this lady ran up to what was left of the car, and our daughter told her to call mom and gave her the phone number.

It only took Charlotte 4 minutes to get to the accident. She jumped out of the car and ran to Angela as they were lifting the Semi-Truck off of the car and were using the "Jaws of life" trying to get both girls out. They got Angela out first and were putting her in the ambulance as Charlotte ran over there, and jumped into the ambulance with her, and the look on Charlotte's face was, *"Don't tell me to leave, because I am not leaving."* The paramedics were trying to put on a neck brace, but Angela was fighting them and they could not put it on. They looked up at Charlotte, not knowing what to do. She told them to strap Angela down. Then told Angela to let them put on the neck brace. With mom there, Angela knew that everything was going to be ok. As they were going to the hospital, the paramedics could hear Charlotte quoting scriptures.

"Be careful for nothing; but in every thing by prayer and supplication with thanksgiving let your requests be made known unto God. And the peace of God, which passeth all understanding, shall keep your hearts and minds through Christ Jesus."

Philippians 4:6-7

When the ambulance showed up at the trauma unit and they wheeled her inside; that was when I showed up. I will never forget the words that Angela said to me. *"Dad, am I okay from the neck down? Are my legs okay?"*

I said, *"Well, honey, besides the blood gushing out your ears and you snapped your jaw in half in two places, you're fine!"*

She looked up at me and said, *"Good, get me up and let's go home!"*

And then she looked at mom and said, *"Do we still have to go to church tonight?"*

"No, honey!"

"Good," she said, *"I am so tired."*

And Charlotte whispered into her ear, *"Rest Honey, just rest."*

As the trauma unit doctors were showing up; they told me to get out and looked at Charlotte and said, *"But you can stay!"* I think they must have heard what happened in the ambulance, or saw the look in my wife's eyes.

I would rather fight a grizzly bear than mess with

my wife when she gets that determination look.
Doctors from all over started showing up; they said
the eye socket was crushed and Angela was seeing
double vision. And the next thing I knew, an eye
doctor was there asking me if he could go in and
make sure that her eyes were ok! Then two more
doctors, some of the best plastic surgeons, just happened to be there and heard of the wreck. And then
a neurologist just happened to be passing through.
God had every doctor there within seconds. With
all of the injuries that Angela sustained, the right
doctors were there. They all told me later that it was
a miracle that they were right there, perfect timing.
But we all know of God's perfect timing.

The other girl was not doing well at all. She was
still trapped in the car. And because of the massive
brain damage, they called in Life Star. They finally
got her out and flew her to the same trauma – unit.
At the time they did not know who the other girl's
parents were. They put her in the room next to us.
They asked me who her parents were and if we
could get a hold of them. I asked Charlotte if she
had the mom's number; she told me that she would
call them and get them here.

The other girl slipped into a coma and it would
be months before she would come out of it.

As the DPS officers and the Firemen started
showing up at the hospital to see how the girls were

doing. I asked them what happened. The DPS officers said that the girls pulled up to a stop sign, and stopped. They proceeded to cross the intersection, not seeing a ¾ ton pickup pulling a trailer going about 55 mph which T-boned the passenger side of the car where my daughter was sitting. At that time it knocked the car over the over pass, down the embankment into the path of a semi-truck, which ran over the car and ended up dragging the car about 100 yards with the truck over them!

One of the fireman said there was not one inch of the floor that was not covered in blood.

The bolts inside the car, that held the seats in, were sheared in half that. The passenger side where Angela was, had disintegrated. There was no right side of the car left.

Some of the other firemen showed up at the hospital to tell me they were sorry that Angela did not make it. I told them God works miracles; not only was she alive, she was still talking, broken jaw and all. My dad and mom showed up and began to pray and comfort us. Dad, being a police officer for 27 years, went to look at the wreck and came back saying it was one of the worst wrecks he had ever seen. He said no one should have survived that wreck, especially Angela.

That first 24 hours was touch and go. Angela was in serious condition that first day. But each time I walked into the room, Charlotte was holding Angela's hand and quoting scriptures and reading from the Bible. I had to make Charlotte go home and rest. She never left her Bible; she always had it with her. And that's not all she had with her. Charlotte always had 50 to 100 tracts on how to know for sure that Heaven can be your home. During the 8 days that Angela was in the hospital, I handed out about 150 tracts. But Charlotte handed out about a 1000 tracts. She was known through out the hospital as the "Tract Lady." If a door was not locked, she was opening them and handing out tracts. I had people come up to me asking where the tract lady was, so they could take some more tracts and give them to their family to read. No one at the hospital dared to tell her that she could not hand out tracts. There were a few times that I thought she was going right into the surgery rooms. This lady was not going to be defeated by Satan. I wish I could have seen the Devil and his Angels running and trying to hide from Charlotte in that hospital.

> "Submit yourselves therefore to God. Resist the devil, and he will flee from you. Draw nigh to God, and he will draw nigh to you..."
>
> **James 4:7-8**

Charlotte left no rocks unturned. Satan found out that night that Charlotte never quits or loses her faith in God. It doesn't matter how many times that Satan knocks her down in life, she always gets back up! I have never seen her doubt God, or ask why? She had a prayer that she wanted answered, to heal Angela and the other girl.

"And whatsoever we ask, we receive of him, because we keep his commandments, and do those things that are pleasing in his sight."

1 John 3:22

"Trust in the LORD, and do good; *so* shalt thou dwell in the land, and verily thou shalt be fed. Delight thyself also in the LORD; and he shall give thee the desires of thine heart. Commit thy way unto the LORD; trust also in him; and he shall bring *it* to pass."

Psalm 37:3-5

And God did just that; he healed Angela and God is still working his miracles on the other girl.

"Ask, and it shall be given you; seek, and ye shall find; knock, and it shall be opened unto you: For every one that asketh receiveth; and he that seeketh findeth; and to him that knocketh it shall be opened."

Matthew 7:7-8

Ten

THE DAY OUR
WORLD ENDED

-- 2009 --

As the months went by, Angela's body began to heal up from the wreck. But that is where it stopped; physically she looked fine, but not spiritually. She quit reading her Bible and praying. We both thought it was a passing teenage phase and she would be back to her normal self any day.

With each passing day Angela was pulling further and further away from God and us. And the arguments between us started to heat up.

"Abstain from all appearance of evil."
1 Thessalonians 5:22

The people that she was hanging around with were not Christian young men and women. We began telling her that unless they were Christians, she could not hang out with them. So behind our backs, she was still hanging out with these rebellious kids. And it wasn't long after this, then we began to hear bad things going on.

"...be sure your sin will find you out."

Numbers 32:23

Her attitude began to get worse and worse. We tried grounding and forbidding Angela to run around with them. We dug in for a hard fight and Angela dug in, too. The battle was on! And we lost!

The day Angela ran off was a day that all of our hopes and dreams for her came to an end. It was like someone took a knife and kept stabbing us in our hearts, over and over again. I have had broken ribs, a dislocated shoulder, blew my knee out, broken fingers and have had my jaw knocked out of place. But that pain was nothing compared to the pain we had in our souls. Satan was back! And he came back with vengeance. Satan delivered a blow to our family that knocked us all down. Charlotte was the first to get back up, and began to pray. I stayed knocked down and anger was my comfort. It was what I thought could make my pain go away.

The minutes turned into days, and days turned into weeks and weeks turned into months. Angela wandered into darkness, just like the "Prodigal Son.

"And he said, A certain man had two sons: And the younger of them said to *his* father, Father, give me the portion of goods that falleth *to me.* And he divided unto them *his* living. And not many days after the younger son gathered all together, and took his

journey into a far country, and there wasted his substance with riotous living.

Luke 15:11-13

Satan told Angela that the world is like a big
party. Satan made it look like fun, with no consequences; a life of freedom, where there are no rules,
and anything you want, you can have.

Satan is the ruler of darkness where each time he
can cause a child of God to fall, is just another trophy
in his showcase. Satan's goal is to destroy families.

"...for he is a liar, and the father of it."

John 8:44

Satan tells our children that the world is for their
taking, just reach out and take what you want, be
anything you want to be, and that the only thing in
this world that matters is yourself.

"...enjoy the pleasures of sin for a season;"

Hebrew 11:25

The world is mean, where love turns into lust,
and happiness turns into sadness, where light turns
into darkness, where fun turns into hurt and pain,
and freedom turns into bondage.

As the days went by, Charlotte kept telling me
that God is in control and is still working. She never

lost hope that Angela would come home. We both began to pray as a team. And our family and friends began to pray that no matter what it took, God would bring Angela back home.

But what happened next was that we began to have people come up to us and tell us that they knew what we were going through. I never really knew the pain and hurt that Satan has caused in this world, until people would tell us their stories of our loved ones that had fallen into sin and darkness.

We learned that when people are hurting, don't leave them to themselves. Go to them, tell them you love them and you are praying for them. And if you have gone through what they have, tell them how you made it, how you survived. Tell them that God is not far away but he is there for them, to comfort, to love, and he is a God that answers prayers.

Because of Charlotte's faith in God and never giving up, my anger turned into love and prayers with every breath. Prayer never left our lips; we prayed morning, noon and night and never stopped praying for Angela. We would wake up in the middle of the night, wondering where she was and if she was ok! And the only comfort came through praying and reading the Bible, and God telling us that He is still in control.

Just like his prodigal child began to see the way of the world was not what he thought, and Satan came to collect his dues. Angela soon began to see that her real friends were the Christian ones.

> "And when he had spent all, there arose a mighty famine in that land; and he began to be in want. And he went and joined himself to a citizen of that country; and he sent him into his fields to feed swine. And he would fain have filled his belly with the husks that the swine did eat: and no man gave unto him."
> **Luke 15:14-16**

During this time of trials and tribulation, an old preacher friend of ours, Dr. James Wilkins came through town. So we met and had lunch together and he began to ask us what our plans were. I looked at Charlotte and asked, *"What plans?"*

He said, *"In serving God!"* This old preacher told me, *"I know you are running from his calling."* I looked at Charlotte and she knew that also. But we have a daughter that has just run away and you are talking about a calling and commitment! WOW! Did I get a preaching to! It turned into who is in control, you or God! *"There is not much time left, before the rapture,"* he said.

Satan has knocked my family down but, not out! This preacher is right; Satan has gotten me sidetracked. Just like he fooled Angela; he had fooled me.

The look on Charlotte's face when I told her, *"I'm*

back!" was a smile that came across her lips. Now we are back up, fighting Satan. He had hurt us badly and now it was time to hurt him.

So I got back into my studies and finally received my Bachelor's degree in Theology and Master's in Christian Ministry Now am working on my Doctorate degree.

And a lot of situations began to happen to Angela. Everything that could go wrong did. When it became some of the darkest days for her, Angela would call mom. Charlotte was always there for her, not in a way that Charlotte would give her money, but in a way that only a mom and a daughter could understand.

Angela had fallen and Satan was not letting her up. But through a lot of prayers and Charlotte's faith of never giving up, Satan was beginning to lose his grip.

> "And when he came to himself, he said, How many hired servants of my father's have bread enough and to spare, and I perish with hunger! I will arise and go to my father, and will say unto him, Father, I have sinned against heaven, and before thee, And am no more worthy to be called thy son: make me as one of thy hired servants."
>
> **Luke 15:17-19**

More answered prayers, some good and some bad, but Angela was beginning to see just how Satan fooled her.

She began to look to mom for guidance and strength. Angela began to grow and mature with wisdom that was handed down by "Hard-Knocks."

"It took the love of a mother and the patience of Job to wait upon the Lord to move in Angela's life." My mom said.

"And he arose, and came to his father. But when he was yet a great way off, his father saw him, and had compassion, and ran, and fell on his neck, and kissed him. And the son said unto him, Father, I have sinned against heaven, and in thy sight, and am no more worthy to be called thy son. But the father said to his servants, Bring forth the best robe, and put *it* on him; and put a ring on his hand, and shoes on *his* feet: And bring hither the fatted calf, and kill *it*; and let us eat, and be merry: For this my son was dead, and is alive again; he was lost, and is found. And they began to be merry."

Luke 15:20-24

Just like the Prodigal Son that came back; so did our daughter. Even though she has to pay for her sins on earth, we serve a living God that forgives, and can turn bad into good.

"And we know that all things work together for good to them that love God, to them who are the called according to *his* purpose."

Romans 8:28

* * * * * * *

It is God's provision that brings the victory.

"Not that we are sufficient of ourselves to think any thing as of ourselves; but our sufficiency *is* of God;"

2 Corinthians 3:5

As we focus on the sufficiency of God and remember and scripturally use the positional and delegated power and authority of our Lord Jesus Christ, we walk in victory.

Victory hinges upon your focus. The mind that is stayed upon God has peace. But by the same principle, the mind that is distracted from God loses peace. The peace that passeth understanding is stablished, strengthened and settled ground that enables us to be steadfast, unmovable, always abounding in the work of the Lord, which is walking in victory.

Defeat also hinges on your focus. If you take your eyes off the Lord, you soon become like Peter and begin to sink into the waves of trouble the enemy wants you to focus on. Our victory walk rests in maintaining our vessel identity and focusing on the enabling power of the Lord Jesus Christ. The scriptures clearly show this.

Basic Training in Spiritual Warfare
by Ed Bausell

"But we have this treasure in earthen vessels, that the excellency of the power may be of God, and not of us. *We are* troubled on every side, yet not distressed; *we are* perplexed, but not in despair; Persecuted, but not forsaken; cast down, but not destroyed; Always bearing about in the body the dying of the Lord Jesus, that the life also of Jesus might be made manifest in our body."

2 Corinthians 4:7-10

"Wisdom is not knowledge itself, but knowing what to do with the knowledge we have."
Bible Doctrines by, M.R. Matthews

eleven

THE REST OF THE STORY

In 2009, I totally surrendered to the Lord to do and go wherever God wanted. As I wanted to be a preacher, I had no idea what was next. If it were not for a pastor like Dr. Wilkins who took time to mentor and guide me on how to fully surrender and then guide me in the right direction, I would still be seeking God's will. In 2011 Dr. Wilkins introduced me to Dr. McMath who kept encouraging me to be ordained as a Preacher. With the backing of these two men of God, and 13 other Pastors and Missionaries, I was Ordained January, 2012 and sent out of Valley Bible Baptist Church to preach God's word.

As for Charlotte, by now you know that she never gets left behind when it comes to serving the Lord. For five years I had been praying that she would help me in the jail Ministry. Every week I would go preach to the men, I would walk by the women's Pods and see that they had no hope in their eyes. But for five years Charlotte would tell me that she was scared and would not know what to say. Charlotte was letting fear creep back into her life, that old giant was back, like David who faced Goliath, Charlotte had her giant to face. The week

I was ordained, I went up to Charlotte like I have so many times before and began telling her again that those women in jail needed her. They need a mom that many of them never had, they needed someone that would not judge them, someone to love them and tell them of the love of Christ. I told her she is a preacher's wife now and that when God called me, God also called her. I will never forget the smile that came across her face and the words that came next, the words that I have been waiting to hear for five years. Charlotte said "Ok, what do I need to take," not what do I say to those ladies, for God was already giving her the words to say. With her Bible in one hand and gospel tracts in the other hand, she was walking out the door to fight that giant again. As she passed me by, I saw a look of a warrior in her eyes; a look that I have seen many times before while I was in the Marine Corp. When faced with fear, these men would call out to an almighty God and ask for boldness to not let fear hold them back. Charlotte was ready for battle. She was going into the lion's den, not knowing what would happen or if they would accept her or would they even listen to her? With only her Bible and some tracts, I sent her into maximum security women's pod. The guards locked Charlotte up in a little cell with 12 women and left the room. Charlotte was all by herself, or was she? When David faced Goliath, he was not alone, God was right there with him. Charlotte was not alone; she felt the comfort of the Holy Spirit taking over. All God wanted was Charlotte to be willing to go, with a boldness that only comes from Him. Charlotte began telling the women that even if the world has given up on them, Christ has not. For the next hour, she told them how Christ loved them so much that he died on the Cross and shed his blood for their sins that they might have eternal life. When her time was over, 9 women received Christ as their Lord and Savior and 3 rededicated their life. When I got through preaching to the men and got back into the office, there was Charlotte with a smile of victory. God led her into battle and with the power of Christ, that giant was defeated. Since then, Charlotte has gone every week with me. There has been days where some of those women are hurting and they lash out with anger and yell and cuss at Charlotte and say they hate God. But when they see Christ's love through Charlotte and begin to listen to her quoting and reading God's Word, that anger and hate turns into tears as they realize that God loves them no matter what.

About a year ago a woman came up to me and asked me if I was the author of the book "Silent Warrior." She wanted to know how Angela and Daniel were doing. I told her that I am so proud of Angela. She is in her second year of College, studying to be a teacher for special needs children. And she is working full time and taking 9 semester hours and faithful in church. As for her son, that's another story. Daniel is a Tom Sawyer, Huckleberry Finn and Dennis the Menace all rolled up into one. He is everything that we prayed for in a grandson. Charlotte and I would not change one thing. Daniel is three years old now and God is going to do great and mighty things in his life. He is such a blessing in all of our lives. May we learn to see through his eyes, not a world that is falling apart but a world of hope and dreams. May we have the faith of a child knowing that God is always there and everything is going to be ok. May we keep our eyes each day focused on Christ.

God Bless,
Richard, Charlotte, Angela and Daniel. Matt. 22:37

Twelve

MEMORIES OF FRIENDS

Charlotte is one of those unique individuals whose friendship one cherishes because within a very short time of knowing her, you know that she is a genuine Christian person. She shows her love and walk with our Lord in so many ways. No matter what the problem, be it hers or yours, she meets it head on as a challenge that will be accomplished for the best. That is of course because she will take it to our Lord and will follow through. You can depend on Charlotte to do what she says she will do. I am blessed to have her friendship. When I have a special need in my life, I will call upon her, my Christian warrior, to accompany me in taking it to our Lord.

Love and Prayers,
Donnis Oakley

* * * * * *

Charlotte loves friends,

"A friend loveth at all times…"

Proverbs 17:17

"A man *that hath* friends must shew himself friendly…"

Proverbs18:24

When my husband Curtis and I met Charlotte and her husband Richard in 1982, we became friends right away; we were members of the same church. We would get together after church and play Monopoly or Scrabble. It was always a lot of fun. But then we moved away after a couple of years and lost contact. Several years later my husband decided he would try their old phone number. Sure enough they answered, and we have been friends for over twenty five years now. Charlotte truly is a friend that shows herself friendly. I could call her any time of the day or night and she would be there to listen. What I've known about Charlotte from the beginning is that she accepted Christ into her heart when she was a child. So she has always had a close walk with the Lord. She not only walks the walk but she talks the talk. She loves to tell others about Christ, and hand out tracts with her husband. We call each other all the time for prayer requests for something or someone in our lives. I know when I ask, she will pray. It's a good feeling to know she is true friend. Charlotte is shy, but strong in her faith. Quiet and understanding, willing to listen to any problem, and not point her finger; she truly does strive to be Christ like. Other than pleasing God first, she truly wants to please her husband. I am very thankful for my friendship with Charlotte. And I pray that God will continue to bless her and use her in a mighty way. Philippians 4:9 those things which ye have both learned, and received, and heard and seen in me, do: and the God of peace shall be with you. This is my friend, Charlotte.

My Friend in Christ,
Lynn Bailey

* * * * * * *

I met Charlotte Girl as a member of Central Baptist Church. I found out later she started there on the nursery roll; I will not give you the year. Though Charlotte Girl can always remember my age, and she asks me each year to make sure I remember.

Charlotte Girl has been my Christian friend for many years and has always been there when I needed a prayer warrior, Bible verses, or just someone to giggle with, when no one else would think it funny.

I attended church most of my life but, I do not know if I would have ever started soul winning or making needed church visits if it were not for her.   And that is how she got the name Charlotte Girl.   The first time I made church visits was because of her. I loved my Pastor who is now deceased, he kept encouraging us to make visits and invite someone to church.   Charlotte Girl asked that I go with her one Tuesday morning; if you have not gone door knocking or witnessing, I encourage you to find "your Charlotte Girl" and ask to go with her. Look for an avid soul winner with a sweet spirit that can convert that stomach full of butterflies to a stomach full of giggles.

You see, Charlotte Girl understands what a lot of Christians are missing out on in life and that is having a merry heart, while doing the Lord's work. She shows how an understanding heart and smile can help struggling sinners make a decision for Christ, get back in Church, keep a unborn baby from going to an abortion mill, or just to keep a smile and know all is well.

Charlotte does not dress like your average Preacher's wife in high heels, but wears sandals most of the time, not just for doing a lot of walking and while witnessing for the Lord but also to run through every water sprinkler or every water puddle that she finds, while talking about what the Lord has done, and will do, or giving the needed scripture all before your next visit! Charlotte Girl keeps a merry heart even when we passed the address of our visit, turn around start laughing about her mistake and pass the same address again.

On our Women's fellowships retreats, she will stay up all night testifying about the Lord and His great works and be the first one to the roller coaster if it is at an amusement park. She will eat burned hot dogs during picnics, all the time laughing and planning what trail to go hiking on. In the middle of our Church picnic when a water balloon toss started, there is Charlotte Girl, keeping her testimony but laughing at every toss and who might get hit.

Hence the name, Charlotte Girl, for her child like happiness and love of the Christian Life!

What a testimony! God help us to be more like Charlotte Girl.

Your sister in Christ,
Donna Smith

* * * * * * *

Charlotte, do remember the time that my pick-up was stolen? And we called the Sheriff Dept. to report it. We had not seen each other for ten years. So we had a lot of catching up to do. I remember we had some errands to run. I parked my truck and jumped into your car. Later that day we came back to get my truck, and could not find it. We looked all over the parking lot, still no truck. And while I was making out the stolen vehicle report in this deputy's patrol car, you remembered that I parked it at this other place of business. Such a blonde moment! We laughed all the way to your house.

Love and Prayers,
Karen Montgomery

* * * * * * *

Charlotte, you make me feel young again, and turn my pain into laughter. Your mom was my best friend. And when I am talking to you, it reminds me of all the loving memories we shared with your mom.

Remember the time you took me to the doctor and then Wal-Mart to get my medicine. My bursitis was acting up, and I could not walk very well. So you talked me into driving one of those electric carts. It was my first time; you said it was easy, just press down on the petal to go. So I pressed down on the petal and off I went, right into a display, knocking it over, and then almost ran over this little boy. The look on that little boys face, as this crazy old lady was coming at him and you yelling and laughing at me to stop. When I finally stopped, and turned around and saw you laughing so hard and you could barely walk. I burst out laughing too. Everybody made it out alive that day. Charlotte, I had so much fun with you that day.

Your old friend in Christ,
Mary Gomez
(1922-2009)

* * * * * * *

When I think of encouraging, strong, bold, diligent, confident and quick, Charlotte's is the face I see. She is just overflowing with scripture for every and in any circumstance. I have yet to ask her anything that she did not know the answer. God displays wonderful knowledge in her. She can whip that sword out quicker than anyone I have met. I love her assurance and her zeal. She just shines with happiness and peace that passes all understanding that only Christ can give.

Your friend in Christ,
Crysta Sullivan

* * * * * * *

I have gone to church with Charlotte and her family for several years at Arden Road Baptist Church. However, my personal relationship with her has really developed over the past three years.

In March 2007, we both joined a new program at the church called Reformers Unanimous, which is a faith based addictions and discipleship program. I joined because I had a deep desire to grow in my relationship with the Lord. Charlotte and I were placed in the same ladies group and within a short period of time I was the group leader and Charlotte was my helper. This was a totally new role for me as I had never led anything before in my life. Charlotte seemed to gently take me under her wing. Not only did she help with group discussion in the class, but she would also pull me aside and point out verses and viewpoints that I hadn't recognized in class. She would even give me verses that showed me how my viewpoint on a topic wasn't correct. She quickly became a very important spiritual mentor to me.

She has so much knowledge of the word that it challenges me to this day to dig deeper, study harder, and memorize more verses. I can sit beside her in Sunday school, hear the teacher mention a verse, and Charlotte will quote it or know where it's located. We have also taken several classes together through our church, including Kirk Cameron's "Way Of The Master" witnessing program. Spreading the gospel and reaching souls for Christ is Charlotte's passion. As a part of the class, we have served in various events, handing out tracts. This is something that I am still working at getting more comfortable with; however, this is second nature to Charlotte. In fact, she doesn't just hand out tracts at church events, she hands them out almost everywhere she goes such as the mall, Wal-Mart, gas stations, etc. She even does it when she goes out of town. In 2008, she invited me to go with her to a ladies retreat in Louisiana. Every stop we made, Charlotte would give me a handful of tracts and we would pass them out to people. Notice I said we handed them to people. Charlotte didn't do what I would have done which is put them on a car window or in the bathroom stall. No. She actually walked up to people, smiled, and handed the tract to them. Out of all the stops we made that trip and the many people we encountered, we only had one person be rude and unkind. She taught me that most people won't bite if you try to simply hand them a tract.

Charlotte has not only been a spiritual mentor and challenged me, but she has also been a true friend... In February 2009, my family encountered a very difficult and scary situation. Due to those events, I missed a class on Tuesday and choir practice on Wednesday. By Friday, Charlotte was calling and asking if everything was ok and if she could come see us. There wasn't anything she could do to fix the situation, but she was a friend. She was there for us. She listened. She cared and she prayed for us. Charlotte is a friend that is also very trustworthy. I have been able to share, discuss, and receive advice from her on things that were very private. I knew that I could trust her to keep confidentiality and not gossip with others. I also knew she would tell me the truth even if it hurts, to hear it.

In addition, Charlotte has been a testimony to me through her own godly living. I have watched her go through some very difficult and trying situations. She reacted by patiently enduring, praying, reading God's Word, and standing on His promises. She never complained or questioned God on why things were happening that way. She simply went to her Heavenly Father and allowed Him to work. Prayers weren't answered over night, but in His timing, God answered those prayers and blessed her.

In summary, Charlotte is a very dear and special person that I hold close to my heart. She has a genuine heart and is a true friend who mentors, encourages, challenges, teaches, loves, and cares for others. I thank God for placing her in my life. She has been a blessing. May God richly bless her in return.

My mentor in Christ,
Ginnie Grant

* * * * * *

We met Charlotte Little (now Ashford) in 1973 in Amarillo, TX in Central Baptist Church. She was a teenager who never failed to attend a service in the church. After a time my husband, John, and I taught the young people's Sunday school class in which Charlotte was enrolled. No matter what the project or the work that needed to be done, Charlotte was always willing to help and was the most faithful student we had. She was a quiet, shy young lady, but always working and always wanting to be a blessing to others. Charlotte and Richard were the first couple that we discipled. Charlotte began to flourish, opening up like a rosebud becoming a flower. She has witnessed, overcoming her shyness, to anyone she has met. Her burning desire was, and is, to see people saved from hell and serving the King. She has risked embarrassment and ridicule to share Christ with others. She and Richard are still discipling new converts, because they have captured the vision of Christ, a global vision. No one that has gotten to know Charlotte has ever had a negative word to say about her. She has been one of the greatest encouragements to me (and to many others) during all the years of our friendship. There is no place too far to go and no effort too great to put forth to see someone saved. She has a rare gift from the Lord for unconditional love. She loves the unlovable, comforts the undeserving and prays "without ceasing" for them. She is the epitome of the edifier that the Lord commands us to be. In times of her own trials and adversities, Charlotte has turned to God's Word and has used the times of refining to glorify the Lord, telling others how wonderful and comforting her Father is. She has demonstrated that she truly believes God's Word as it is written during these difficulties. Not only does Charlotte believe the Bible; she has memorized an amazing number of verses and passages from the Scriptures because she loves the Word of her Father. I believe with all my heart that during the millennial reign of Christ, Charlotte will be sitting at the feet of Jesus, right along with the apostles and the Marys of the New Testament. She can never get enough of Jesus. I am blessed to call her my friend, my sister and prayer warrior. I thank the Lord for her and for her love for Him and for people.

Your sister in Christ,
Wanda
Missionary to Mexico

Thirteen

CONCLUSION

I hope the story of Charlotte, has encouraged you and brought you one step closer to the Lord. Charlotte starts her day by praying and reading her Bible; and ends her day the same way. That is why she is known as the "Silent Warrior." When her family and friends need someone to pray, they call Charlotte. And through her silent prayers, she takes those requests unto the Lord with a child-like faith, and believes all things are possible. She prays for the will of God to be done. There may be storm clouds in your life, and all seems dark, but remember Christ is behind those clouds waiting to shine through, if you let Him!

We are going to leave you with some scriptures, and if you feel overwhelmed, angry or just need comforting, read and memorize these scriptures. As Christ used scriptures to defeat the Devil, we can use scriptures to resist and defeat and overcome the Devil and draw closer to Christ.

Dr. Wilkins said to me once, *"Saturate yourself with the Word of God."*

God's Promises
Anger

"Let all bitterness, and wrath, and anger, and clamour, and evil speaking, be put away from you, with all malice: And be ye kind one to another, tenderhearted, forgiving one another, even as God for Christ's sake hath forgiven you."

Ephesians 4:31-32

"Be ye angry, and sin not: let not the sun go down upon your wrath:"

Ephesians 4:26

Charity

"Give, and it shall be given unto you; good measure, pressed down, and shaken together, and running over, shall men give into your bosom. For with the same measure that ye mete withal it shall be measured to you again."

Luke 6:38

"And now abideth faith, hope, charity, these three; but the greatest of these *is* charity."

1 Corinthians 13:13

Comfort

"Come unto me, all *ye* that labour and are heavy laden, and I will give you rest."

Matthew 11:28

Courage

"I can do all things through Christ which strengtheneth me."

Philippians 4:13

Death

"Yea, though I walk through the valley of the shadow of death, I will fear no evil: for thou *art* with me; thy rod and thy staff they comfort me."

Psalm 23:4

Enemies

"So that we may boldly say, The Lord *is* my helper, and I will not fear what man shall do unto me."

Hebrews 13:6

Eternal Life

"For the wages of sin *is* death; but the gift of God eternal life through Jesus Christ our Lord."

Romans 6:23

Faith

"Now faith is the substance of things hoped for, the evidence of things not seen."

Hebrews 11:1

"Knowing that a man is not justified by the works of the law, but by the faith of Jesus Christ, even we have believed in Jesus Christ, that we might be justified by the faith of Christ, and not by the works of the law: for by the works of the law shall no flesh be justified."

Galatians 2:16

"I have fought a good fight, I have finished *my* course, I have kept the faith:"

2 Timothy 4:7

Faithfulness, God's

"For ever, O LORD, thy word is settled in heaven. Thy faithfulness *is* unto all generations…"

Psalm 119:89-90

Fear

"For God hath not given us the spirit of fear; but of power, and of love, and of a sound mind."

2 Timothy 1:7

Forgiveness

"But I say unto you, Love your enemies, bless them that curse you, do good to them that hate you, and pray for them which despitefully use you, and persecute you; That ye may be the children of your Father which is in heaven: for he maketh his sun to rise on the evil and on the good, and sendeth rain on the just and on the unjust."

Matthew 5:44-45

Gospel

"For I delivered unto you first of all that which I also received, how that Christ died for our sins according to the scriptures; And that he was buried, and that he rose again the third day according to the scriptures:"

1 Corinthians 15:3-4

Gossip

"Keep thy tongue from evil, and thy lips from speaking guile."

Psalm 34:13

Grace, Saving

"For by grace are ye saved through faith; and that not of yourselves: *it is* the gift of God: Not of works, lest any man should boast."

Ephesians 2:8-9

Grace, Growth in

"But the path of the just *is* as the shining light, that shineth more and more unto the perfect day."

Proverbs 4:18

"But grow in grace, and *in* the knowledge of our Lord and Saviour Jesus Christ. To him *be* glory both now and for ever. Amen."

2 Peter 3:18

Guidance

"For this God *is* our God for ever and ever: he will be our guide *even* unto death."

Psalm 48:14

"In all thy ways acknowledge him, and he shall direct thy paths."

Proverbs 3:6

Guilt

"If we confess our sins, he is faithful and just to forgive us *our* sins, and to cleanse us from all unrighteousness."

1 John 1:9

"As far as the east is from the west, *so* far hath he removed our transgressions from us."

Psalm 103:12

Help in Troubles

"They that sow in tears shall reap in joy. He that goeth forth and weepeth, bearing precious seed, shall doubtless come again with rejoicing, bringing his sheaves *with him*."

Psalm 126:5-6

"The LORD *is* my rock, and my fortress, and my deliverer; my God, my strength, in whom I will trust; my buckler, and the horn of my salvation, *and* my high tower."

Psalm 18:2

Holy Spirit

"And I will pray the Father, and he shall give you another Comforter, that he may abide with you for ever; *Even* the Spirit of truth; whom the world cannot receive, because it seeth him not, neither knoweth him: but ye know him; for he dwelleth with you, and shall be in you."

John 14:16-17

"Likewise the Spirit also helpeth our infirmities: for we know not what we should pray for as we ought: but the Spirit itself maketh intercession for us with groanings which cannot be uttered. And he that searcheth the hearts knoweth what *is* the mind of the Spirit, because he maketh intercession for the saints according to *the will of* God."

Romans 8:26-27

Hope

"Who by him do believe in God, that raised him up from the dead, and gave him glory; that your faith and hope might be in God."

1 Peter 1:21

"The wicked is driven away in his wickedness: but the righteous hath hope in his death."

Proverbs 14:23

"Which *hope* we have as an anchor of the soul, both sure and stedfast ... Jesus ..."

Hebrews 6:19- 20

Humility

"...Wherefore he saith, God resisteth the proud, but giveth grace unto the humble."

James 4:6

"A man's pride shall bring him low: but honour shall uphold the humble in spirit."

Proverbs 29:23

Job, well done

"His lord said unto him, Well done, *thou* good and faithful servant: thou has been faithful over a few things, I will make thee ruler over many things: enter thou into the joy of thy lord."

Matthew 25:21

Joy

"They that sow in tears shall reap in joy. He that goeth forth and weepeth, bearing precious seed, shall doubtless come again with rejoicing, bringing his sheaves *with him*."

Psalm 126:5-6

"Yet I will rejoice in the LORD, I will joy in the God of my salvation."

Habakkuk 3:18

"For our heart shall rejoice in him, because we have trusted in his holy name."

Psalm 33:21

"Rejoice in the Lord alway: *and* again I say, Rejoice."

Philippians 4:4

Life Verse, Charlotte's

"And let us not be weary in well doing: for in due season we shall reap, if we faint not."

Galatians 6:9

Loneliness

"Then shalt thou call, and the LORD shall answer; thou shalt cry, and he shall say, Here I *am*..."

Isaiah 58:9

"And will be a Father unto you, and ye shall be my sons and daughters, saith the Lord Almighty."

2 Corinthians 6:18

Long Life

"Ye shall walk in all the ways which the LORD your God hath commanded you, that ye may live, and *that it may be* well with you, and *that* ye may prolong *your* days in the land which ye shall possess."

Deuteronomy 5:33

"My son, forget not my law; but let thine heart keep my commandments: For length of days, and long life, and peace, shall they add to thee."

Proverbs 3:1-2

Love, Brotherly

"Beloved, if God so loved us, we ought also to love one another."

1 John 4:11

"By this shall all men know that ye are my disciples, if ye have love one to another."

John 13:35

Love, God's

"For God so loved the world, that he gave his only begotten Son, that whosoever believeth in him should not perish, but have everlasting life."

John 3:16

"I am crucified with Christ: nevertheless I live; yet not I, but Christ liveth in me: and the life which I now live in the flesh I live by the faith of the Son of God, who loved me, and gave himself for me."

Galatians 2:20

"My sheep hear my voice, and I know them, and they follow me: And I give unto them eternal life; and they shall never perish, neither shall any *man* pluck them out of my hand. My Father, which gave *them* me, is greater than all; and no *man* is able to pluck *them* out of my Father's hand."

John 10:27-29

Loving God

"Delight thyself also in the LORD; and he shall give thee the desires of thine heart."

Psalm 37:4

"But as it is written, Eye hath not seen, nor ear heard, neither have entered into the heart of man, the things which God hath prepared for them that love him."

1 Corinthians 2:9

"Henceforth there is laid up for me a crown of righteousness, which the Lord, the righteous judge, shall give me at that day: and not to me only, but unto all them also that love his appearing."

2 Timothy 4:8

Lust

"For all that *is* in the world, the lust of the flesh, and the lust of the eyes, and the pride of life, is not of the Father, but is of the world. And the world passeth away, and the lust thereof: but he that doeth the will of God abideth for ever."

1 John 2:16-17

"Submit yourselves therefore to God. Resist the devil, and he will flee from you. Draw nigh to God, and he will draw nigh to you. Cleanse *your* hands, *ye* sinners; and purify *your* hearts, *ye* double minded."

James 4:7-8

Lying

"A faithful witness will not lie: but a false witness will utter lies."

Proverbs 14:5

Marriage

"For this cause shall a man leave his father and mother, and shall be joined unto his wife, and they two shall be one flesh."

Ephesians 5:31

"That they may teach the young women to be sober, to love their husbands, to love their children, *To be* discreet, chaste, keepers at home, good, obedient to their own husbands, that the word of God be not blasphemed."

Titus 2:4-5

Meekness

"To speak evil of no man, to be no brawlers, *but* gentle, shewing all meekness unto all men."

Titus 3:2

"Blessed *are* the meek: for they shall inherit the earth."

Matthew 5:5

Money

"He that trusteth in his riches shall fall: but the righteous shall flourish as a branch."

Proverbs 11:28

Patience

"And let us not be weary in well doing: for in due season we shall reap, if we faint not."

Galatians 6:9

Peace

"Thou wilt keep *him* in perfect peace, *whose* mind is stayed *on thee*: because he trusteth in thee."

Isaiah 26:3

"And the peace of God, which passeth all under-standing, shall keep your hearts and minds through Christ Jesus."

Philippians 4:7

Prayer

"If ye abide in me, and my words abide in you, ye shall ask what ye will, and it shall be done unto you."

John 15:7

"And whatsoever we ask, we receive of him, because we keep his commandments, and do those things that are pleasing in his sight."

1 John 3:22

"Evening, and morning, and at noon, will I pray, and cry aloud: and he shall hear my voice."

Psalm 55:17

Pride

"Pride *goeth* before destruction, and an haughty spirit before a fall."

Proverbs 16:18

Protection, God's

"When thou liest down, thou shalt not be afraid: yea, thou shalt lie down, and thy sleep shall be sweet."

Proverbs 3:24

"I will both lay me down in peace, and sleep: for thou, LORD, only makest me dwell in safety."

Psalm 4:8

"The LORD *is* my light and my salvation; whom shall I fear? the LORD *is* the strength of my life; of whom shall I be afraid?"

Psalm 27:1

Righteousness

"But seek ye first the kingdom of God, and his righteousness; and all these things shall be added unto you."

Matthew 6:33

"For the kingdom of God is not meat and drink; but righteousness, and peace, and joy in the Holy Ghost."

Romans 14:17

Salvation

"For God so loved the world, that he gave his only begotten Son, that whosoever believeth in him should not perish, but have everlasting life."

John 3:16

"For whosoever shall call upon the name of the Lord shall be saved."

Romans 10:13

Seeking God

"And they that know thy name will put their trust in thee: for thou, LORD, hast not forsaken them that seek thee."

Psalm 9:10

Self-Righteousness

"Woe unto *them that are* wise in their own eyes, and prudent in their own sight!"

Isaiah 5:21

Shame

"Let my heart be sound in thy statutes; that I be not ashamed."

Psalm 119:80

Shine

"Let your light so shine before men, that they may see your good works, and glorify your Father which is in heaven."

Matthew 5:16

"And they that be wise shall shine as the brightness of the firmament; and they that turn many to righteousness as the stars for ever and ever."

Daniel 12:3

Sickness

"For I will restore health unto thee, and I will heal thee of thy wounds, saith the LORD…"

Jeremiah 30:17

Success

"By humility *and* the fear of the LORD *are* riches, and honour, and life."

Proverbs 22:4

"This book of the law shall not depart out of thy mouth; but thou shalt meditate therein day and night, that thou mayest observe to do according to all that is written therein: for then thou shalt make thy way prosperous, and then thou shalt have good success."

Joshua 1:8

"But his delight *is* in the law of the LORD; and in his law doth he meditate day and night. And he shall be like a tree planted by the rivers of water, that bringeth forth his fruit in his season; his leaf also shall not wither; and whatsoever he doeth shall prosper."

Psalm 1:2-3

Trust

"Trust in the LORD, and do good; *so* shalt thou dwell in the land, and verily thou shalt be fed. Delight thyself also in the LORD; and he shall give thee the desires of thine heart. Commit thy way unto the LORD; trust also in him; and he shall bring *it* to pass."

Psalm 37:3-5

"Trust in the LORD with all thine heart; and lean not unto thine own understanding. In all thy ways acknowledge him, and he shall direct thy paths."

Proverbs 3:5-6

Wisdom

"If any of you lack wisdom, let him ask of God, that giveth to all *men* liberally, and upbraideth not; and it shall be given him."

James 1:5

Word of God

"Blessed *is* he that readeth, and they that hear the words of this prophecy, and keep those things which are written therein: for the time *is* at hand."

Revelation 1:3

"Being born again, not of corruptible seed, but of incorruptible, by the word of God, which liveth and abideth for ever... But the word of the Lord endureth for ever. And this is the word which by the gospel is preached unto you."

1 Peter 1:23, 25

Worry

"Be careful for nothing; but in every thing by prayer and supplication with thanksgiving let your requests be made known unto God. And the peace of God, which passeth all understanding, shall keep your hearts and minds through Christ Jesus."

Philippians 4:6-7

"But my God shall supply all your need according to his riches in glory by Christ Jesus."

Philippians 4:19

Worship

"O come, let us worship and bow down: let us kneel before the LORD our maker."

Psalm 95:6

Our desires ought to be, what God's desires are. As Christ prayed, *"Not my will, but thine, be done,"* should be our goal. Each day is a battle, some harder than others. But each day, look up to God for guidance and ask forgiveness for our past, and don't look back. May your life be full of victories and someday walk those streets of gold and see face to face, our Lord and Saviour, and hear those precious words, *"Well done thou good and faithful servant."*

"These things I have spoken unto you, that in me ye might have peace. In the world ye shall have tribulation: but be of good cheer; I have overcome the world."

John 16:33

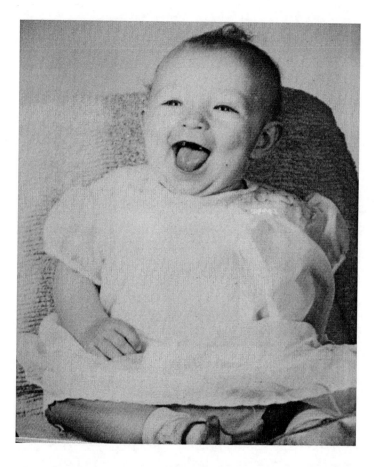

This is Charlotte when she crawled into the closet
and found the whiskey bottle and looked up at
Mama and said, "DaDa!"

Charlotte when she said, "I was not an accident, I
was a surprise!"

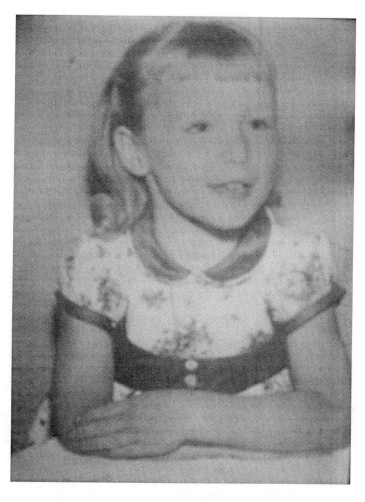

Pogo Stick story.

USMC I am the one in the middle, front row, we all
looked like skeletons.

USMC story.

This is Michael our son.

The whole family, top row: Me, and Mama, bottom
row: my dad and mom, Charlotte and Angela .

Daniel, our handsome grandson. (Romans 8:28)

THE NEXT SILENT WARRIOR!